Second Edition

Achieve
IELTS 1

English for International Education

Intermediate–Upper Intermediate   Band 4.5–6   CEFR B1–B2

Workbook with Audio CD

Caroline Cushen
Susan Hutchison
Louis Harrison

Achieve IELTS 1 Intermediate–Upper Intermediate Workbook, Second Edition
Caroline Cushen, Susan Hutchison & Louis Harrison

Publisher: Gavin McLean

Senior Commissioning Editor: John Waterman

Editorial Project Manager: Karen White

Content Project Editor: Tom Relf

Developmental Editors: Sarah Warren and Lynn Thompson

Head of Production and Manufacturing: Alissa McWhinnie

Strategic Marketing Manager: Charlotte Ellis

Production Controller: Elaine Willis

Compositor: MPS Limited, a Macmillan Company

Cover design: George Rigopoulos

Audio produced by The Soundhouse Studio, London

Media Researcher: Victoria Townsley-Gaunt

ISBN: 978-1-133-31386-1

National Geographic Learning
Cheriton House, North Way, Andover, Hampshire, SP10 5BE
United Kingdom

Cengage Learning is a leading provider of customized learning solutions with office locations around the globe, including Singapore, the United Kingdom, Australia, Mexico, Brazil and Japan. Locate your local office at: **international.cengage.com/region**

Cengage Learning products are represented in Canada by Nelson Education, Ltd.

Visit National Geographic Learning online at **ngl.cengage.com**
Visit our corporate website at **www.cengage.com**

We are grateful to the following for permission to reproduce copyright material:

Mousetrap Media Ltd for an extract on page 30 from 'Starting out as a media journalist', www.journalism.co.uk, copyright © Mousetrap Media Ltd; Guardian News and Media Ltd for an extract on page 43 from 'UN report: World's biggest cities merging into 'mega-regions'' by John Vidal, 22/03/2010, copyright © Guardian News and Media Ltd 2010; Office for National Statistics on page 45 for the table 'Leisure activities in British cities by age' adapted from Social Trends, Office for National Statistics, © Crown copyright; Professor Eric H. Chudler for material on page 48 adapted from 'Yawning' by Eric Chudler, faculty.washington.edu/chudler/yawning.html, reproduced with permission; Barnardo's for an extract and their company logo on page 60, www.barnardos.org.uk, reproduced with permission; Shelter for an extract and their company logo on page 60, www.shelter.org.uk, reproduced with permission; WaterAid for an extract and their company logo on page 60, www.wateraid.org, reproduced with permission; RNLI for an extract and their company logo, on page 60, www.rnli.org.uk, reproduced with permission; Oxfam for an extract and their company logo on page 61, www.oxfam.org.uk, reproduced with permission; Guardian News and Media Ltd for extracts on page 60 and 76 adapted from 'Q&A: How to become a volunteer' by Patrick Butler, *The Guardian* 1 June 2005, and Guardian News and Media Ltd for an extract adapted from 'Worried about losing your memory?' by Phil Hogan, *The Guardian*, 15 June 2003, copyright © Guardian News and Media Ltd 2003, 2005; and Home Office for material on page 95 adapted from "Your Practical Guide to Crime Prevention" © Crown Copyright 2000.

In some instances we have been unable to trace the owners of copyright material and we would appreciate any information that would enable us to do so.

Cover Credits: Shutterstock/Andresr, Shutterstock/Goodluz, Shutterstock/lightpoet, Shutterstock/Omer N Raja.
Inside Photo Credits:
Alamy/Travel Pictures p16, Alamy/Richard Wadey p25(c), Alamy/ilian studio p25(d), Alamy/AF archive p28(t), Alamy/Sam Edwards p51(t), Alamy/DCPhoto p56, Alamy/blickwinkel p57(b), Alamy/Art Directors & TRIP p64(b), Alamy/Cultura Creative p64(t), Alamy/Justin Kase z11z p65(br), Alamy/incamerastock p70;
Corbis/Atlantide Phototravel p14(t), Corbis/PAUL YEUNG/Reuters p25(e), Corbis/Raf Makda/VIEW p41, Corbis/CHRISTOPHER JUE/epa p46(t), Corbis/Studio DL p57(2), Corbis/Image Source p57(3), Corbis/Robert Michael p57(4), Corbis/Limelight-Studio/Westend61 p57(5), Corbis/Jens Wolf/dpa p57(6), Corbis/Pete Saloutos pp61, 58, Corbis/Buero Monaco/zefa p75;
Getty Images/Artifacts Images p10, Getty Images/John Giustina p12, Getty Images/Andersen Ross p21(t), Getty Images/Alex Mares-Manton 25(r), Getty Images/TommL p36, Getty Images p57(7), Getty Images/Max Paddler p65(l), Getty Images p62, Getty Images/Les and Dave Jacobs p72(t), Getty Images/Chris Ryan p76, Getty Images/Don Bayley p78(t);
THE KOBAL COLLECTION/BBC/TRADEMARK FILMS p30(bl), THE KOBAL COLLECTION /BBC/TRADEMARK FILMS p30(br);
Masterfile p57(1);
Photolibrary/Pixtal Images p6(t), Photolibrary/Westend1 p25(l), Photolibrary/Steve Silver p57(t);
Photos.com/Jupiterimages p28(b);
Press Association Images/Dargent Vincent/ABACA p25(a), Press Association Images/Elise Amendola/AP p25(b);
Rex Features/Goldwyn/Everett p30(bm);
SCIENCE PHOTO LIBRARY/PATRICK LANDMANN p42, SCIENCE PHOTO LIBRARY/SIMON FRASER p45;
Shutterstock/fotohunter p40(t), Shutterstock/mart p53, Shutterstock/Vladimir Mucibabic p57(8), Shutterstock/mangostock p71;
SuperStock/Imagebroker.net p20, SuperStock/SOMOS p22, SuperStock/Blend Images p34(t).

Printed in the United Kingdom by Ashford Colour Press Ltd.
Print Number: 04   Print Year: 2022

MIX
Paper from responsible sources
FSC
www.fsc.org
FSC® C011748

Contents

Map of the book

Language study	Pronunciation	Study skills
present continuous present simple	syllables	remembering vocabulary
prepositions of direction	stressed and unstressed syllables	keeping a vocabulary notebook
talking about the future *will /going to*	final /l/ *must(n't)/don't have to*	revising vocabulary
narrative tenses suggestions	numbers	using a dictionary
present perfect; giving reasons	acronyms	choosing correct meanings from a dictionary
present passive	/ɜː/, /ɔː/, /ʌ/, /ʊː/	dictionary work
comparatives and superlatives	weak forms in comparatives	grouping
real conditionals; *in case, unless*	real conditionals	resources in libraries
should(n't), must(n't); possibility and certainty	*should(n't), must(n't)*	using illustrations and diagrams
relative clauses	sentence stress	collocation
second conditional	second conditional	collocation with *make* and *do*
gerunds and infinitives	*-ing*	exam preparation

Unit 1

On course

IELTS tasks: matching headings and paragraphs; multiple-choice questions

1 Choose the most suitable headings for paragraphs A–G from the list of headings. There is one extra heading.

1	The Australian lifestyle	_____	**5**	Misunderstandings	_____
2	First day	_____	**6**	An exciting moment	_____
3	Changing places	_____	**7**	A new campus	_____
4	Feeling homesick	_____	**8**	Just like home	_____

A new life

A Last year I exchanged my job as a lecturer in a British university for a post at the University of Queensland for six months. When I finally landed in Australia, the first thing I noticed was how relaxed and friendly the people were, unlike those at the airport at Heathrow. I suppose that's because there are far fewer of them.

B On the first day, I woke up to bright sunshine, early in the morning. I could hear loud birdsong of a type I had never heard before, and somebody laughing very loudly near my window.

I later found out that it was a kookaburra! Although it was March, the beginning of winter in Australia, the temperature had gone up to thirty degrees by the time I got to the breakfast table. This was the first time I had met up with my new colleagues, and found them to be very helpful and welcoming, although I didn't much like being greeted as *the new Pom*.

C Walking to the Languages Department, I was struck by the beauty of the gardens and the types of flowers and plants which grew there. Students were sitting around on the grass, chatting or reading, some catching up with a late breakfast before the lectures began. New students were heading for the Admissions Department to enrol.

D As students, however, they are pretty much the same as the ones back home. They turn up to the wrong lectures, forget their books and pens, fall asleep in class and stay up all night having parties. I felt that I was on familiar ground when I held my first tutorial.

E What did I enjoy most? I think it was the outdoor lifestyle, with picnics and barbies even in the winter. Even events such as weddings and birthday parties are often held in the open air. Australians love to get together and have a good time.

F And the greatest problem? For me, it was the language. It took me some time before I could get used to the local accent and get to the meaning, because the vowel sounds are so different from British English. But by the time I left, I could understand perfectly. When I first got back to England, my colleagues even told me I sounded like an Aussie myself.

G Taking up an opportunity like this is something I would certainly recommend. I have wonderful memories of fantastic wildlife, beautiful beaches and endless sunshine. My best memory of all is of skydiving: jumping out of a plane at 2500 metres over the gorgeous Lockyer valley. I never would have plucked up the courage to do that in England!

 **Check your answers.**

2 Now read the passage again and choose four letters A–G.

1 While she was in Australia, the lecturer …
   A noticed that the people were less stressed than in England.
   B felt very hot and uncomfortable.
   C didn't like being called a *Pom*.
   D thought the students were lazier than in England.
   E went to an outdoor wedding.
   F learned to understand Australian English.
   G tried a new sport.

 Check your answers.

3 Match the Australian words with the definitions.

1 *barbie*   A a kind of bird
2 *Pom*   B an English person
3 *kookaburra*   C an Australian
4 *Aussie*   D a barbecue

 Check your answers.

Vocabulary

1 Label the diagrams. Use these words.

line graph   bar chart   flow chart   table   pie chart

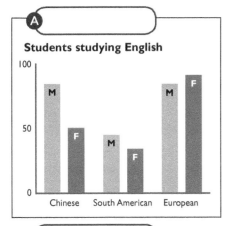

A

Students studying English

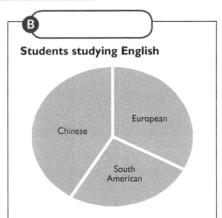

B

Students studying English

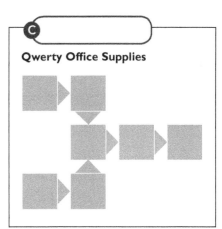

C

Qwerty Office Supplies

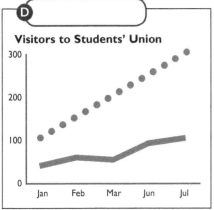

D

Visitors to Students' Union

E

Students in Department of Business

	Economics	MBA	Accounting
2007	139	59	132
2008	145	62	138
2009	122	50	127
2010	152	64	140
2011	161	72	146
2012	165	68	151

 Check your answers.

2 Match the sentences to diagrams A–E. Then complete the sentences using these words. You may use the words more than once.

rows   segment   columns   horizontal axis   vertical axis

1 Diagram _____ is a flow chart. It shows the management structure of the Qwerty Office Supplies company.

2 Diagram _____ is a table of student numbers in the business department. There are three _____ showing the different schools within the department, and six _____ for the past six registration periods.

3 Diagram _____ is a line graph. The _____ shows the number of visitors to the Students' Union, and the _____ shows the months of the year.

4 Diagram _____ is a pie chart. It shows the different nationalities of students studying English in the language department. The largest _____ shows the percentage of Chinese students.

5 Diagram _____ is a bar chart. This shows the same information as the pie chart, but has separate _____ for male and female students.

 Check your answers.

3 Complete the chart.

noun	verb	adjective
admission		
	administer	
	enrol	
registration		

 Check your answers.

4 Complete the information in the prospectus. Use these words.

medicine   biology   agriculture   computing   engineering
business   art and design   languages   architecture

UNIVERSITY DEPARTMENTS

The largest department at the university is now the **(1)** _____ school, where students from all over the world study marketing, accounting and finance.

The university has a working farm, where students of **(2)** _____ can learn the latest methods of growing fruit and vegetables.

Those who are interested in designing the buildings of the future will find the very best tutors and facilities in our excellent school of **(3)** _____.

Many talented painters and sculptors graduate from our **(4)** _____ department.

In our IT department, we have up-to-date hardware and software, with sufficient PCs for classes of up to 50 students of **(5)** _____.

Our **(6)** _____ department has excellent facilities for the study of plants and animals, which we collect from all over the world.

Those who wish to study **(7)** _____ can expect to learn the CAD programme for design and construction of aircraft and other machines. This department has its own racing car, which is maintained by the students.

In the department of **(8)** _____, students can learn German, French, or Spanish as part of their main degree programme. This department also runs a Foundation Course for foreign language speakers studying English.

Next year, the university plans to open a modern school of **(9)** _____, which will be associated with the nearby Addington Hospital for the training of doctors and nurses.

 Check your answers.

1 Look at the picture and answer the questions.

1 What is the student doing?
2 Where is he standing?
3 What do students do there?

 Check your answers.

2 🎧 **1** Listen to the conversation and circle the letters A–D.

1 What is Hiroko doing?
   A Waiting for a phone call.   C Eating lunch.
   B Looking at her timetable.   D Paying for the course.

2 Simon phoned Hiroko because . . .
   A he hasn't got a timetable.   C he wants to discuss the timetable.
   B he wants to have lunch.   D he is going to a lecture.

3 Simon wants to go to the Business School because . . .
   A there is a lecture at 2.00 the next day.   C there is a meeting at ten.
   B Hiroko can get a timetable there.   D it is near the Finance Office.

4 Before they go to the Business School . . .
   A they are going to register.   C Simon is paying for the course.
   B Hiroko is paying for the course.   D they are going to the canteen.

 Check your answers.

3 🎧 **1** Listen again and complete the timetable.

Monday *a.m.*	Tuesday *a.m.*	Wednesday *a.m.*

Registration	Time: **(1)** _____
	Welcome meeting
	Place: Business School,
	    room **(2)** _____
		Time: 10–10.30
		Talk on sports facilities by head
		    of Students' Union
		Place: SU office

p.m.	*p.m.*	*p.m.*
Registration	Time: 14.00 The **(3)** _____ of England Place: Grantham **(4)** _____ Theatre	Free for **(5)** _____

 Check your answers.

Pronunciation syllables

1 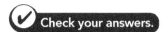 **2** Listen to sentences 1–10. Count the words in each of the sentences. (Count contractions as full words, e.g. *I'm* = *I am* two words.)

1 ___ 2 ___ 3 ___ 4 ___ 5 ___ 6 ___ 7 ___ 8 ___ 9 ___ 10 ___

✓ **Check your answers.**

 **2** Now listen again, and practise each of the sentences.

2 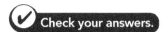 **3** Listen and complete the names, places, email and website addresses. For email and website addresses, use these symbols.

@ (*at*); \ (*backslash*); . (*dot*); / (*forward slash*); : (*colon*)

1 Professor _____

2 Academic writing: _____

3 Address: _____

   _____

   _____

4 Tutor's email: _____

5 Accommodation in _____ Building.

✓ **Check your answers.**

3 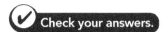 **4** Listen and practise saying the names and addresses.

present simple

1 **Look at the registration form and complete the conversation.**

The University of Arundel
 	
Registration form
	Title: *Mr*
	
	Forename 1: *Anthony*
	
	Forename 2: *Frederick*
	
	Surname: *Jones*
	
	Date of Birth:
	  31st August, 1993
		Nationality: *Australian*
		
		Permanent home address:
		  15 Prospect Road,
		  Adelaide 2145
		  Australia
		
		Term time address:
		  Room 38
		  Harvey Building
			Programme:
			  Business Studies
			
			Personal Tutor:
			  Dr Frances Robinson
			
			New/continuing student?
			  New

Registrar: Good morning. Would you like to register at the University?

Anthony: Yes, please.

Registrar: Good. What is your first name, please?

Anthony: (1) _____

Registrar: Do you have any other forenames?

Anthony: (2) _____

Registrar: And what is your surname?

Anthony: (3) _____

Registrar: Jones. OK. What is your date of birth, Anthony?

Anthony: (4) _____

Registrar: And your nationality?

Anthony: (5) _____

Registrar: Good. What is your home address?

Anthony: (6) _____ ?

Registrar: Yes, I mean the address where your parents live.

Anthony: (7) _____

Registrar: Fine. Where are you staying during term time?

Anthony: (8) _____

Registrar: Which degree programme are you taking?

Anthony: (9) _____

Registrar: Do you have a personal tutor yet?

Anthony: (10) _____

Registrar: Ah, yes. Dr Robinson. One last question: are you a new student or are you continuing from last year?

Anthony: (11) _____

Registrar: Thank you, Anthony. Welcome to Arundel.

Anthony: (12) _____?

Registrar: The Finance Office is on the other side of the park, next to the Great Hall.

Anthony: Thank you very much. Goodbye.

✔ **Check your answers.**

present simple and present continuous

2 **Look at the picture and complete the conversation. Use the verbs in brackets in present simple or present continuous tense.**

Karl: Hi. **(1)** _____ you _____ (wait) to register?

Rosanna: Yes, I am. I suppose you **(2)** _____ (do) the same thing?

Karl: That's right. I **(3)** _____ (wait) to enrol for the Law School.

Rosanna: What's your name?

Karl: I'm Karl.

Rosanna: And I'm Rosanna. Where **(4)** _____ (come) from, Karl?

Karl: I **(5)** _____ (come) from Austria. How about you?

Rosanna: Korea.

Karl: What course **(6)** _____ (enrol) for, Rosanna?

Rosanna: I'm a second year student at the Medical School. I **(7)** _____ (study) psychology this year. Oh, there's Gina! Hi Gina, let me introduce you to Karl. He **(8)** _____ (register) for the Law School.

Gina: Hi Karl. Listen, Rosanna. What **(9)** _____ (do) later on?

Rosanna: I **(10)** _____ (not know), why?

Gina: Well, there's a welcome concert in the Main Hall tonight. **(11)** _____ (want) to come?

Rosanna: Yes, why not. Karl, **(12)** _____ (go) to the concert?

Karl: You bet! The Big Noise **(13)** _____ (play) tonight. They're my favourite band.

Gina: Great! I **(14)** _____ (meet) the others outside the Main Hall at half past eight. See you there.

Rosanna: See you.

✓ **Check your answers.**

Study skills   remembering vocabulary

1 **Look at the words for one minute. Then, close your book and write the words you can remember.**

house bird piano tutor book bursar cat dictionary far elbow
photograph mini-skirt finger magazine accommodation near room
key video enjoy long business lecture agree rooms

Now compare your list with the words in the book. How many did you remember?

2 **Look at your list again, and answer the questions.**

1 Did you write words with similar meanings together, such as *accommodation* and *rooms*?

2 Did you write *far* next to its opposite *near*?

3 Did you notice that *enjoy long business lecture* can be put together to make an idea?

4 Did you group together the types of book that are in the list?

5 Did you remember *mini-skirt*? Why?

6 Did you make a picture in your mind, using some of the words together?

Now tick the techniques you used to remember the new words.

1 remember new words with similar meanings ☐

2 remember the new word and its opposite word ☐

3 put words together to form an idea ☐

4 remember groups of words ☐

5 make a picture in your mind that included the words ☐

1 Look at the charts and complete the sentences.

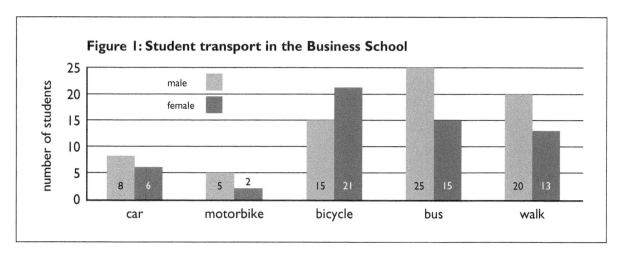

Figure 1: Student transport in the Business School

Figure 1 is a **(1)** _____ chart, which shows the different forms of **(2)** _____ used by students in the **(3)** _____ School. The most popular form of transport for male students is the **(4)** _____, and in the case **(5)** _____ females it is the **(6)** _____.

The least popular form of transport is the **(7)** _____.

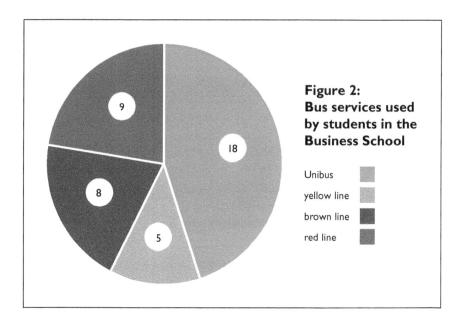

Figure 2: Bus services used by students in the Business School

Unibus
yellow line
brown line
red line

The **(8)** _____ chart in figure 2 shows how many students use the different **(9)** _____ services. The largest **(10)** _____ shows that most of these students use the **(11)** _____ service, while the **(12)** _____ is the least popular, as only **(13)** _____ students use it regularly.

 Check your answers.

Unit 2

Campus

1 Read the passage and complete the diagram. Use these words.

> university   kindergarten   junior high school   BSc   high school
> elementary school   high school diploma   master's degree   gap year

| 1 | 2 | 3 junior high school | 4 | 5 | 6 | 7 | 8 | 9 |

EDUCATION IN CANADA

Most children in Canada start kindergarten at the age of five, but in Ontario only, children start junior kindergarten at the age of four. Elementary school then starts at age six and continues until the age of 12. At this age, children then progress to junior high school and then to high school at the age of 14, where it is compulsory to stay until the age of 16. Many children however, stay until they are 18, particularly in the states of Ontario and New Brunswick where this is compulsory. State schools are free, and education is compulsory for all children. They are usually co-educational, which means that boys and girls are taught together.

At the age of 18, students take the high school diploma and they then leave school. The high school diploma is necessary for any student who

wants to join a university. For less academic students, there are colleges where students can study vocational subjects and gain certificates or diplomas. There are also private career colleges where students can study a specific area such as Information Technology.

Students who attend university will study for a degree. They are accepted from the age of 18, although many now choose to take a 'gap year', delaying the start of university to go travelling. A first degree – Bachelor of Arts (BA) or Bachelor of Science (BSc) – normally takes between three and five years of full-time study. Some students may also go on to study for two years on a master's degree programme. Those who want to reach the highest level of study will take a doctorate.

Check your answers.

2 Do the statements below agree with the information in the reading passage?

Write   TRUE if the statement is true according to the passage.
         FALSE if the statement is false according to the passage.
         NOT GIVEN if the statement is not given in the passage.

1 Canadian families don't have to pay for elementary school.   _____
2 Most children leave school at 16.   _____
3 Most schools are co-educational.   _____
4 Students prepare for the high school diploma at junior high school.   _____
5 Students need a high school diploma to join a university.   _____
6 Many students delay the start of their degree to go travelling.   _____
7 A master's degree takes longer than a bachelor's degree.   _____
8 It takes six years in total to get a doctorate.   _____

✔ Check your answers.

3 Make a list of the similarities and differences between education in Canada and in your country.

Listening   IELTS tasks: note completion, multiple-choice questions

1 🎧 **5** Listen to the talk about private schools in Canada and complete the notes. Use these words.

| boarding school | fees | kindergarten | public school | single sex | government funded | private |

State education is **(1)** _____. Schools which do not rely on government money are called
(2) _____ schools. A **(3)** _____ is a place where the pupils eat and sleep, as well as study.
Children can start boarding school at age five in **(4)** _____. Upper Canada College is a famous
(5) _____. A school for girls only is **(6)** _____. If you want to send your children to a private
school, you have to pay **(7)** _____.

2 🎧 **5** Listen again, and decide which statements are correct. Circle three letters A–F.

A There are fewer students in classes at private schools.
B Private schools are not popular with politicians.
C People who live abroad can send their children to a boarding school.
D Students often need to pass an examination before attending a public school.
E Children can only go to boarding school when they are 13.
F All public schools teach boys and girls together.

✔ Check your answers.

3 🎧 **6** Listen and complete the Campus Tour form.
Write one or two words or a number for each answer.

✔ Check your answers.

Campus Tour

1	Length of tour	_____
2	Campus tour time	_____
3	Maximum number of people	_____
4	Name	_____
5	Start point	_____

Pronunciation stressed and unstressed syllables

1  **7** Listen and count the number of syllables.

> between – *2 syllables* students refectory enjoying sunbathing silly
> laughing towards opposite university – *5 syllables*

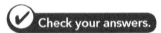 **7** Now listen to the words again, and underline the part of the word which is stressed.

(✔) Check your answers.

2 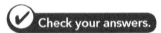 **8** Listen to the recording, and put the words into groups.

> union religious atmosphere several civic admissions bursar
> private government postgraduate workstation lecture

1 Oo **2** oOo **3** Ooo **4** oOoo

private

Now answer the questions.

1 Which is the most common stress pattern?

2 Can you think of at least one more word for each group?

(✔) Check your answers.

Language study prepositions of direction

1 Underline the words in the passage for prepositions of direction.

Example: *Lily walked <u>across</u> the field.*

It was a beautiful day, and most of the students were out enjoying the good weather. Some were sitting talking or sunbathing, others were rowing boats or swimming in the lake. Paul walked towards the lake, climbed up the steps of the boathouse and dived into the water. Lily watched him swim. Feeling hot, she moved into the shade of the trees. From there, she could see the students walking along the path to the refectory.

Paul finished his swim and got out of the water. He came towards her.

'That was great,' he said. 'Why don't you have a swim?'

'I'd rather take a walk,' Lily replied.

'Come on, let's go across the fields to the town. I want an ice cream.'

'OK,' said Paul, 'I'll put on my shirt.' They walked through the trees together, and past the boathouse.

When they came to the gate, Paul jumped over it, but Lily stopped in front of it when she saw a cow walking across the field.

'Paul!' she said, 'Wait for that cow to go away.'

Paul said, 'Don't be silly, Lily. It's only a cow.'

Then the cow passed between Paul and Lily, and she ran towards him, laughing. They walked on, up the hill to the town.

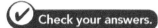 **Check your answers.**

Now complete the sentences. Use the words in the box below.

across   towards   into   in front of   past   across   up   into

He left the examination hall and got **(1)** _____ the car, which was waiting **(2)** _____ the road on the other side.

When she reached the halls of residence, she walked **(3)** _____ the stairs to her bedroom on the second floor.

He picked up the books and put them **(4)** _____ his bag.

The students walked **(5)** _____ the refectory without stopping, then turned **(6)** _____ the bookshop.

I've just seen Paul standing **(7)** _____ the Phoenix Building.

They ran **(8)** _____ the square because they were late for the meeting.

2 Complete the paragraph about where the student goes.

The student goes down the stairs and across the square. Then he . . .

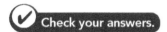 **Check your answers.**

Vocabulary

1 Use words from the box to complete the sentences.

radio station   Student Information Centre   auditorium
art gallery   nightclub   cinema   student IT centre
Bursar's Office   International Office   lecture hall

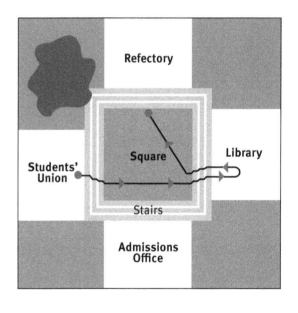

1 The place where students pay their fees may be called the Finance Office or the _____.

2 The largest part of a theatre, where people sit to watch a play or a film, is called the _____.

3 Some universities may have an _____ where students and staff can show their paintings and sculpture.

4 Foreign students can get advice about visas and legal requirements from the _____.

5 For general enquiries about University life, go to the _____.

6 Larger classes often take place in a _____.

7 Students may send emails from the _____ centre.

8 Students who are lucky enough to have a _____ on campus can go there to dance the night away.

9 Many universities now have their own _____ where students can watch the latest films from around the world.

10 Universities which have a _____ can give their students practical experience in reporting, news broadcasting and DJing.

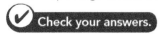 **Check your answers.**

2 Complete the diagram with words and phrases about the Virtual Campus.

wireless network   radio station   modem   workstation   toolbox   workshop
webcam   video conferencing   text book   server   cluster room   pencil case

 Check your answers.

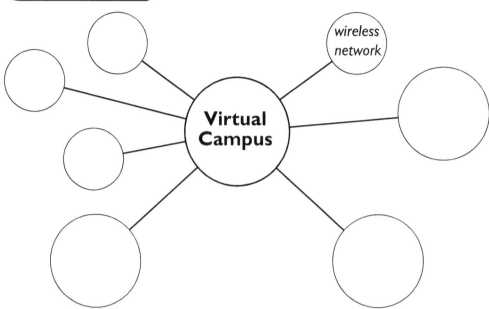

wireless network

Virtual Campus

Writing IELTS tasks: describing charts; general training module task 1

1 Match the phrases below with 1–5.

a sharp rise   a gradual fall   a levelling off   a slight increase   a dramatic fall

 Check your answers.

2 Read the writing task and underline the key words.

> You have just started a course at university. You have left your MP3 player in a hotel you stayed in for two days when you first arrived.
>
> Write a letter to the hotel manager. In your letter …
>
> • explain your situation
>
> • say where you left the MP3 player
>
> • tell the manager what you would like him/her to do
>
> You should write at least 150 words. You do NOT need to write your own address.
>
> Begin your letter *Dear Sir/Madam, …*

 Check your answers.

1

2

3

4

5

Now put sentences A–I in the correct order.

Dear Sir/Madam,

A Last week I stayed in your hotel for two days, on the 11th and 12th of September. ☐ I

B I think I left it in the hotel, in room 101. ☐

C I look forward to receiving my MP3 player. ☐

D I was staying in London on my way to Lancaster University, where I have just started a course in engineering. ☐

E This is on the first floor of your hotel, on the right at the top of the stairs. ☐

F When I arrived at the campus, I unpacked my bags and found that my MP3 player was missing. ☐

G I would be very grateful if you could return my MP3 player to me by post. ☐

H I think I might have left it on the top shelf of the wardrobe, next to the bed. ☐

I I have enclosed an addressed label and enough stamps to cover the cost of postage. ☐

 Check your answers.

3 Choose the most suitable ending for the letter.

Lots of love, Raymond   Best wishes, Raymond   Yours faithfully, Raymond Chan

 Check your answers.

4 Match the salutations with the situations.

1 Dear Sir/Madam,   A You know the person's sex, but not their name.

2 Dear Annie,   B You don't know this person.

3 Dear Madam,   C This person is a good friend.

4 Dear Mrs Radduch,   D You know this person's name, but you are not friends.

 Check your answers.

Study skills keeping a vocabulary notebook

When you learn new words, you should keep a record of them in a vocabulary notebook. There are many ways to do this. Choose the one which you think will work best for you.

1 alphabetical notebook

Buy a notebook with the letters of the alphabet down one side. As you learn new words, transfer them to the notebook. Remember to record what type of word it is (noun, verb, adjective or adverb), the pronunciation, the stress pattern, and to use it in an example sentence. You can write the translation of the word in your language, and include drawings too. You can also keep an electronic notebook in a word processing or spreadsheet programme. Use the format that is most convenient for you.

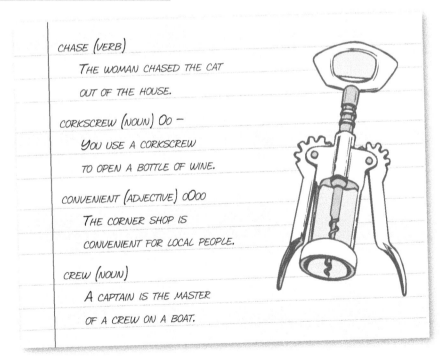

CHASE (VERB)
  THE WOMAN CHASED THE CAT
  OUT OF THE HOUSE.

CORKSCREW (NOUN) Oo –
  YOU USE A CORKSCREW
  TO OPEN A BOTTLE OF WINE.

CONVENIENT (ADJECTIVE) oOoo
  THE CORNER SHOP IS
  CONVENIENT FOR LOCAL PEOPLE.

CREW (NOUN)
  A CAPTAIN IS THE MASTER
  OF A CREW ON A BOAT.

2 topics notebook

You can organise your vocabulary by grouping words together according to the topic. You can use a *spidergram* to do this. Use colours to make the words stand out. You can add new words to the diagram as you learn them.

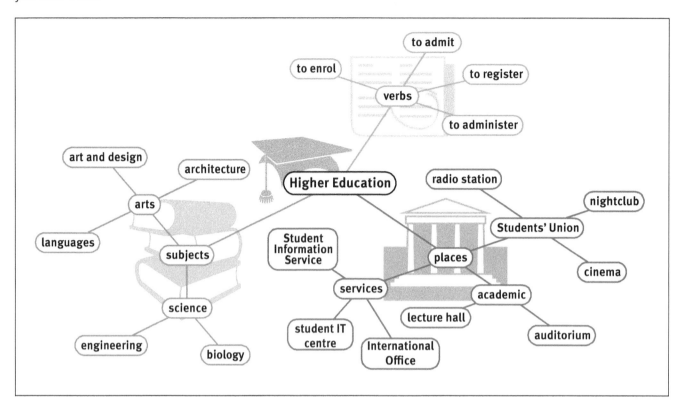

3 card file

Buy a card file index box. As you learn new words, write them down on the cards with the translation on the back of the card. This way you can look through the English words on the cards and remember the translations, or look at the translations and remember the word in English.

Unit 3

Living space

Vocabulary

1 Put the words into groups.

caretaker   corridor   warden   bedsit   flat   kitchen   landlord/landlady
apartment   porter   shared house   hall of residence   security staff   foyer
cleaner   toilet   porter's lodge   flatmate   room mate

1   types of accommodation   **2**   areas in accommodation   **3**   people/jobs

 Check your answers.

2 Decide which words go with these verbs.

washing-up   washing   bed   repairs   vacuuming   ironing   dinner

1   *do*   **2**   *make*

 Check your answers.

Reading   IELTS tasks: multiple-choice questions

1 Read the advertisements and find abbreviations for . . .

1   deposit.   **3**   per calendar month.   **5**   modern conveniences.
2   per week.   **4**   reference.   **6**   bedroom.

 Check your answers.

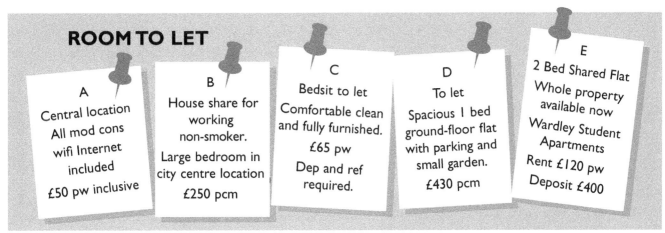

ROOM TO LET

A
Central location
All mod cons
wifi Internet
included
£50 pw inclusive

B
House share for
working
non-smoker.
Large bedroom in
city centre location
£250 pcm

C
Bedsit to let
Comfortable clean
and fully furnished.
£65 pw
Dep and ref
required.

D
To let
Spacious 1 bed
ground-floor flat
with parking and
small garden.
£430 pcm

E
2 Bed Shared Flat
Whole property
available now
Wardley Student
Apartments
Rent £120 pw
Deposit £400

2 Read the advertisements A–E and write the letters of the appropriate advertisements.

Which property is good for . . .

1 a person with a car? _____

2 a person with a computer? _____

3 someone without any furniture? _____

4 a person who doesn't smoke? _____

5 a student with a small family? _____

 Check your answers.

3 Read the passage and answer the questions.

1 Why does Samantha replace keys?

2 Where are most halls of residence?

3 Why do some parents call the department?

4 Which other people work with Samantha?

Student Accommodation

The German student had a problem. 'My mattress is too hard. I have a bad back,' he said. Samantha Black gave the student a form and carefully explained how to fill it in. 'Will you come today with one?' asked the student. Samantha laughed. 'Well, not me – but someone will.' she said.

The question is typical of the problems that many students bring to the University's Student Services Accommodation Department every day. Samantha, the receptionist, gives out keys or replaces those lost or locked in rooms, sorts out post and parking permits, answers questions and offers advice if she knows the answer or directs students to those who do if she doesn't.

Samantha is part of the team that looks after the administration, finance and clerical side of the accommodation service for the 1,900 students who live in the University's halls of residence. Most of the halls are on campus but even those outside are only ten minutes walk away. Students have a choice of single or shared bedrooms, and single sex or mixed floors. They can also opt for smoking or non-smoking rooms.

Once in their accommodation, students continue to visit the Department's reception area with all kinds of requests. They come to collect their mail, meet other students, complain – some come in just for a chat. Samantha also deals with calls from parents worried that they haven't heard from their sons or daughters. 'We either check the room or ask someone to try and find the student and get them to phone home.' she said.

Backed up by a team of wardens, porters and security staff, the accommodation service runs as smoothly as a giant hotel. In the reception area, Samantha Black is trying to find a spare mattress while telling a student where to find the nearest supermarket. 'People think we have the answer to everything,' she said. 'And probably we do.'

Now find words in the passage which mean . . .

1 something to sleep on.

2 a document that allows you to park your car.

3 to choose.

4 to work without problems.

 Check your answers.

Language study talking about the future

will

1 Complete the conversation. Use the verbs in brackets.

A: So, it's 6.00 now and the play **(1)** _____ (start) at 7.30. Susie will meet us in half an hour at reception, then we **(2)** _____ (pick up) Tao outside the internet café 15 minutes later.

B: He **(3)** _____ probably _____ (forget) the time, you know.

A: Well, let's hope he doesn't forget. We **(4)** _____ only _____ (have) enough time to wait for him for five minutes. It **(5)** _____ (take) us about half an hour to get to the theatre.

We **(6)** _____ (see) Istvan outside the theatre at 7.15, he **(7)** _____ (go) there straight from the department. Then I **(8)** _____ (get) the tickets from the box office.

B: It **(9)** _____ (be) too close. Let's go now, then we **(10)** _____ (have) plenty of time and **(11)** _____ (not be) in a rush.

✔ Check your answers.

Now read the conversation again and complete the times.

1 leave hall of residence   _____
2 meet Susie   _____
3 pick up Tao   _____
4 arrive at theatre and see Istvan   _____
5 play starts   _____

✔ Check your answers.

present continuous and will

2 Complete the sentences with the verb in brackets.

1 What _____ you _____ this evening? (do)
   I _____ not _____ anything. I _____ a nice quiet night in watching TV. (do/have)
2 I _____ to London later this week. I _____ you a call nearer the time and let you know when I _____ there. (come/give/be)
3 _____ Turgut _____ tomorrow? (arrive)
   I think so. Then, the next day he _____ to see his other friends in Leeds. (go)

✔ Check your answers.

going to and *will*

3 Complete the sentences with the verb in brackets.

1 The lecture starts in five minutes, and it takes ten minutes to get there. You _____ late. (be)
I think I _____ on my bike, then. (go)

2 Oh dear, it _____ again – look at those clouds. (rain)
We _____ just _____ our waterproof coats. (take)

3 Our lecture for today is cancelled. We _____ it at the end of term. (have)

4 What _____ we _____ about George? He was playing loud music late at night again. (do)
Look, I _____ to him and make sure he doesn't do it again. (talk)

5 How _____ we _____ to France? (get)
I _____ at the map and find the best route. (look)

✔ **Check your answers.**

Pronunciation   final /l/

1 🎧 **9** Listen and notice how the final /l/ in *will* is pronounced.

🎧 **9** Now listen again and practise.

must (n't)/(don't) have to

2 Read the rules and tick *yes* or *no*.

ACCOMMODATION RULES

1 Students must allow University staff to enter the rooms.

2 Students are not allowed to share a single room, or change rooms without permission.

3 At all times, noise must be kept to a low level which does not interfere with the academic needs of other students. During examination periods, noise regulations must not be broken.

4 Parties are allowed with the agreement of the hall warden.

5 Students are responsible for damage to their own rooms and the cost of any repairs will be charged to the student. A deposit of £300 has to be paid.

6 No pets may be kept in University residences. This includes birds and reptiles.

7 Students have to pay for their accommodation before term begins.

	yes	no
1 University staff can enter the rooms.	☐	☐
2 Students can share rooms.	☐	☑
3 Students can make a lot of noise.	☐	☐
4 Students can have parties.	☐	☐
5 Students can have pets.	☐	☐
6 Students don't have to pay for accommodation until the end of term.	☐	☐

✔ **Check your answers.**

3 Look at pictures 1–5 and write sentences.

✔ **Check your answers.**

No Smoking
1

No Loud Music
2

Date for essays –
6th December
3

No Parking
4

No Food and Drink in the Lecture Theatre
5

Study skills · revising vocabulary

1 Label the vocabulary entries. Use these words.

> pronunciation   word type   stressed syllable   example   definition
> key word   words that go together   revised/remembered columns

✓ **Check your answers.**

Now write entries for five more words.

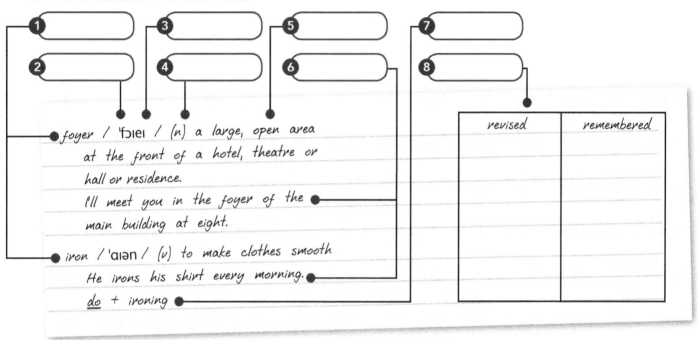

1   3   5   7

2   4   6   8

foyer / ˈfɔɪeɪ / (n) a large, open area at the front of a hotel, theatre or hall or residence.
I'll meet you in the foyer of the main building at eight.

iron / ˈaɪən / (v) to make clothes smooth
He irons his shirt every morning.
do + ironing

revised	remembered

2 Read the texts and answer the questions.

I keep my new words on small cards – one card for each word. That way when I'm on a bus or train, or when I have some spare time, I can take them out and learn them. I have two sets of cards: one set are the words I'm learning at the moment. The other set is words I think I know. I keep the words I'm learning with me all the time. I keep the words I think I know at home, and ask my girlfriend to test me on them every week.

My new words are in my notebook. At the side of them I have two columns. The first column is for words I know – I tick the first when I learn a word and can still remember it one week later. The second column is when I can remember a word one month later – then I'm sure I know it.

1 Which way of revising and remembering do you think is best?

2 How do you revise and remember new vocabulary?

3 Can you think of any more ways of revising and remembering new words?

1 **Read the letter and circle three letters A–E.**

The writer would like . . .

A a road map.

B directions to the shops.

C to know when they can move into the room.

D a cleaner.

E a parking permit.

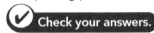 Check your answers.

Dear Ms Black,

Thank you for arranging my accommodation. I will arrive on 26 July but would like to get some further information from you.

Firstly, could you send me a map of the city and the University? As I will drive to the University, a road map and directions will be very useful. Could you also arrange a parking space and permit for me, or advise me how to apply for this?

I would also like to know when I will be able to move into my room and where to collect the keys from.

I look forward to hearing from you.

Regards,

Tao Chen

Now underline the phrases for making requests.

 Check your answers.

2 **Read the task and underline the key words.**

> You are going to start a course at a college in Australia. Write a letter to the admissions tutor. In the letter . . .
> - say when and where you are arriving.
> - explain that you are not familiar with the city.
> - say what you need from the college.

 Check your answers.

Now write a letter of at least 150 words.

1 🎧 **10 Listen to a talk and match the pictures with the categories.**

1	entertainment robot	C
2	appliance robot	☐
3	immobot	☐
4	assistive robot	☐
5	android	☐

✔ Check your answers.

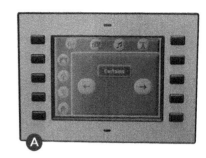
A

2 🎧 **10 Listen again and circle A–C.**

1 The talk is about . . .
  A cleaning.
  B technology in the home.
  C the ageing population.

B

2 Robots are . . .
  A machines with sensors, a microprocessor and artificial intelligence.
  B machines that think like a human.
  C machines that do repeated tasks.

3 The robot dog can . . .
  A use a lot of energy.
  B play games.
  C take photos.

C

4 Immobots are . . .
  A worth $138 billion today.
  B positioned around the house and work as a team.
  C very good alarm clocks.

5 In the next ten years . . .
  A 14% of people will wear a computer.
  B 25% of people will wear a computer.
  C 40% of people will wear a computer.

D

6 Androids are . . .
  A very strong.
  B able to smile.
  C completely life like.

✔ Check your answers.

Now complete the summary. Use these words.

entertainment	chores	housework	categories	ageing	human	team

In the future, robots will do many household **(1)** _____. There are five
(2) _____ of robot. Firstly, **(3)** _____ robots, like toys; secondly,
appliance robots that do the **(4)** _____ we don't want to do. Next,
are immobots – robots that work as a **(5)** _____ around the house.
Fourthly, assistive robots help people with tasks and may be very useful in the
future for an **(6)** _____ population. Finally, androids are **(7)** _____
robots and are the most difficult to build.

E

✔ Check your answers.

Unit 4

Film society

Listening IELTS tasks: table completion

1  **11 Listen to a film star and answer the questions.**

What happened in Harry's life . . .

1 before he met Cindy?
2 while he was in Africa?
3 after he moved to Barbados?
4 one year later?

✔ Check your answers.

2  **11 Listen again, and complete the table with the main events in Harry's life, A–J, in each year.**

1992	*B*	2002	
1993		2006	
1995		2008	
1996		2009	
2001		2010	

A went to Africa
B expelled from Eton
C moved to Barbados
D met Cindy
E met and married Lulu
F made *Hello Saturday*
G married Cindy
H broke his neck
I divorced
J made *Captain Sam*

✔ Check your answers.

narrative tenses

1 The pictures show what happened to Harry Harpoon's first wife, Cindy. Look at the examples and answer the questions.

Lived in Africa, divorced Harry

When did she divorce Harry?
She divorced him while she was living in Africa.
She divorced him before she went to Paris.

Lived in Paris, married Jean-Paul

When did she marry Jean-Paul?
_____
_____ (after)
_____
_____ (while)
_____
_____ (before)

Studied art, won the lottery

When did she win in the lottery?
_____
_____ (after)
_____
_____ (while)
_____
_____ (before)

Worked and brought up children, had art exhibition

When did she have an art exhibition?
_____
_____ (after)
_____
_____ (while)
_____
_____ (before)

Lived in New York, learned to sing

When did she learn to sing?
_____
_____ (after)
_____
_____ (while)
_____
_____ (before)

Sang in nightclub, Jean-Paul left her

When did Jean-Paul leave her?
_____
_____ (after)
_____
_____ (while)

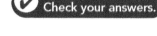
Check your answers.

suggestions

2 Read the conversation and underline the suggestions.

Dona: We need some ideas about a film for tonight. Tao, what are your thoughts on this? Do you have any suggestions?

Tao: How about showing a Kung Fu movie?

Istvan: I'd like to suggest a romantic film. It's nearly Valentine's Day.

Dona: Good idea. Have you got any more suggestions?

Sara: We could show a horror movie.

Dona: I'd like to avoid doing that. Some of them are very violent.

Check your answers.

Now complete the conversation.

Tao: We need to decide on a topic for our project. Do you (1) _____, Catherine?

Dona: We all love martial arts films. (2) _____ writing it on the film industry in China?

Tao: I don't think we could find enough information in the library. Have you got (3) _____?

Dona: Well, we (4) _____ write about two films we know well, and compare them.
       I'd (5) _____ *Enter the Dragon* and *Kung Fu Hustle*. (6) _____ on this?

Tao: I think that sounds interesting. What do you think, Istvan?

 Check your answers.

Reading   IELTS tasks: true/false/not given; general training module

1 Do the statements agree with the information given in the reading passage?

Write   **TRUE** if the statement is true according to the passage.
        FALSE if the statement is false according to the passage.
        NOT GIVEN if the statement is not given in the passage.

1 The castle was in poor condition.   _____

2 They were not a normal family.   _____

3 The castle belonged to the father.   _____

4 The stepmother was a practical person.   _____

5 Cassandra was unattractive.   _____

I Capture the Castle

The main character in this film is Cassandra Mortmain, who lived with her very eccentric stepmother and father, and her beautiful sister, Rose. In the time of his greatest success, after the publication of his first novel, her father rented a castle, where they had been living for the past 12 years. But the castle was falling down because since that time, he had not been able to write a word and the family had no money. The stepmother, Topaz, was an artist and too much of a dreamer to be of any real help to the girls. When their American landlord, Simon, and his brother arrived at the castle, Rose decided to make Simon fall in love with her, and eventually she did. They arranged to get married, and everyone ignored Cassandra in the excitement. However, events did not turn out as predicted, and Cassandra experienced first love and first heartbreak at the same time.

 Check your answers.

2 Now read the passage again, and put the events in order.

- **A** Two Americans came to the castle.
- **B** Unexpected things happened.
- **C** The father published a book.
- **D** Cassandra fell in love.
- **E** The family became poor.
- **F** The father rented a castle.
- **G** Simon fell in love with Rose.

✔ **Check your answers.**

3 Match the paragraphs with the types of film.

1	martial arts	**3**	romance	**5**	comedy	**7**	science fiction
2	thriller	**4**	drama	**6**	horror		

Boa ☐
Deep in the Antarctic, at the most secure prison camp in the world, a group of scientists discovered the remains of a terrifying monster which was still alive. This will make you jump out of your seat.

About Schmidt ☐
Warren Schmidt has retired from his job as an insurance agent. As he writes to a young boy he has adopted, who lives in Tanzania, he wonders about the meaning of his life, and searches to find his true purpose.

Another 24 hours to die ☐
Just as Bill Taylor is going to end all his money problems, he receives a phone call with the terrible news that a bomb has been put inside his body. The voice demands that he carries out a series of surprising tasks which will have you sitting on the edge of your seat.

Solaris ☐
Chris Kelvin was sent to visit a space station on the planet Solaris. When he arrived, he found that the controller had killed himself, and that the other scientists were behaving very strangely. Then he too began to feel the power of the planet. What is the secret of Solaris?

The Accidental Spy ☐
Jackie Chan discovers that he is not going to be a salesman all his life when he finds out that he comes from a family of spies. The story becomes more and more complicated, with plenty of action and Kung Fu, as Chan fans have come to expect.

Along came Polly ☐
Reuben's new wife decides to leave in the middle of their honeymoon, which changes all his plans. Suddenly, his old friend Polly arrives on the scene, looking for laughter, adventure and fun.

Beyond Borders ☐
Until Nick came into her life, Sarah had little to do but go to parties and shop. His career as a caring doctor, and her love for him, made her follow him all over the world – and into great danger.

✔ **Check your answers.**

Vocabulary

1 Complete the sentences. Use these words.

    funds vote treasurer secretary minutes apology committee

1 This person looks after a club or society's money: _____.
2 People meeting together to make decisions are a _____.
3 _____ are notes about the meeting.
4 The _____ is the person who organises the papers.
5 Members of the committee may need to _____ when they cannot agree about something.
6 When you cannot attend a meeting, you should send an _____.
7 The film society can buy a new projector if they raise enough _____.

✔ **Check your answers.**

1 Look at the numbers and decide how many words you need for each number.

> 2,780,923 (*two million, seven hundred and eighty thousand, nine hundred and twenty-three*) = 12 words

A 384,802
B 1,068, 069
C 57,530
D 1,700,836,742
E 9,450,413
F 762,984

 **12** Now listen to the recording and check your answers.

✔ **Check your answers.**

2  **12** Listen again and underline the stressed words.

A three hundred and eighty-four thousand, eight hundred and two
B one million, sixty-eight thousand and sixty-nine
C fifty-seven thousand, five hundred and thirty
D one billion, seven hundred million, eight hundred and thirty-six thousand, seven hundred and forty-two
E nine million, four hundred and fifty thousand, four hundred and thirteen
F seven hundred and sixty-two thousand, nine hundred and eighty-four

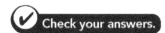 **13** Now listen and practise saying the numbers.

✔ **Check your answers.**

Writing IELTS task: describing a table

1 Read the title, look at the table and answer the questions.

1 Which years is the table about?
2 How many types of film are included?
3 Which film made the biggest profit?

The table shows the amount of money made by the most popular films by type, in 2009 and 2010. Write a report for a university lecturer describing the information shown below.

Genre		2009	2010
Action	profit top film	£1,683,228,954 *Avatar*	£499,280,068 *Inception*
Comedy	profit top film	£282,659,606 *The Hangover*	£619,700,990 *Alice in Wonderland*
Drama	profit top film	£320,351,773 *Inglourious Basterds*	£237,676,627 *The King's Speech*

✔ **Check your answers.**

2 Look at the table in question 1 and put the sentences in order.

A *Alice in Wonderland* made £619,700,990, and *The Hangover* made about £337,000,000 less than that.

B In this category, the least amount of profit was made in 2010.

C This film made a profit of £499,280,068, which is less than a third of the amount made by *Avatar* the year before.

D This table shows the amount of money made by the top films in three genres, in 2009 and 2010.

E The second genre is comedy.

F The first type of film the table shows is action, with the film *Inception*.

G The third and final category is drama.

 Check your answers.

Now write two more sentences about drama using the information in the table.

_____

_____

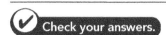 Check your answers.

Study skills using a dictionary

1 You need an English to English advanced learner's dictionary for studying.

Electronic dictionary translations can cause problems for students, as there are so many synonyms – words of similar meaning – in English. Literal translation can only work in very simple sentences. A good learner's dictionary will give you much more information about the word than its meaning.

Read the dictionary entry and find . . .

1 A word-break dot.

2 A phonemic transcript.

3 The part of speech of the word.

4 An abbreviation meaning *especially*.

5 An abbreviation meaning *and so on*.

> stu.dent /stju:dənt/ *n* 1 (a) a person who is studying for a degree, diploma, etc. at a university or some other place of higher education or technical training: a *BA student or a medical student, a student nurse, teacher, etc or student politics.* (b) (*esp US*) boy or girl at school.

 Check your answers.

2 Complete the sentences with the correct word form.

| studio (n)   studious (adj)   study (v)   study (n)   studied (adj) |

1 A _____ person spends a lot of time studying.

2 A _____ can be a room in your house for working in, or a drawing which is done before the main picture.

3 To _____ is to learn from books, etc.

4 A _____ is a place where an artist works, or a TV programme is made.

5 A _____ reaction is carefully planned, not accidental.

✔ Check your answers.

Unit 5

Bulletin

Reading — IELTS tasks: identifying synonyms; true/false/not given

1 Read the passage and find words with similar meanings.

1 journalist _____
2 independent _____
3 important _____

4 sometimes _____
5 jobseekers _____
6 connections _____

Online Journalism News

How to apply for a job – and how not to!

We recently advertised for freelance reporters for this website and received 82 applications in total. Despite publishing several hundred journalism recruitment vacancies every year, we rarely recruit journalists ourselves, so it has been a fascinating insight into how journalists apply for jobs and the mistakes they make.

Here is the original advert, with the key points in bold:

> We are looking for **freelance** news reporters for **occasional news writing** about online journalism for our website www.journalism.co.uk
>
> **You will be located in the UK and have experience in media, business and/or technology journalism, relevant qualifications and a very keen interest in new media.**
>
> Please apply by **emailing CV, links to your work** and an indication of your **approximate fees per story.**
> **Absolutely no calls or agencies.**

All the applications, with one or two exceptions, were from experienced and qualified professional journalists. Most of them would have been capable of doing the job. Somehow we had to filter down the applications, and one way was to examine how well the candidates had responded to the requirements stated in our advert.

*Freelance . . .

Thirteen applicants had full-time jobs, and two were students. As we were looking for occasional reporting, the full-timers were not suitable because they would not be available during normal working hours.

*You will be located in the UK . . .

Six applicants were not.

*Have experience in media, business and/or technology journalism, relevant qualifications and a very keen interest in new media . . .

Forty-eight applicants did not give any information about their knowledge in these areas.

*Please apply by emailing CV . . .

Eleven applicants did not include a CV with their applications. Two CVs were in unreadable formats.

*Links to your work . . .

Thirty-seven applicants did not provide links to their work, something we would expect for an online writing position.

*And an indication of your approximate fees per story . . .

Thirty-one applicants did not give us any information about their charges.

*Absolutely no calls or agencies.

One applicant called the office.

Out of the 82 applicants, we shortlisted six whom we hope to try out in the near future.

When applying for a job, think about these points:

- Think of the advertiser. How many responses are they likely to get, and what makes **you** better than the other applicants?
- Be brief, don't waste their time by writing too much. Make sure that everything you write is relevant to the advertisement.
- Do some research into how much money you should ask for. Don't undervalue your work, but don't ask for too much either.
- If you don't get the job, accept it. You may not be right for this one, but it's quite possible that you are suitable for other work. We have kept all the CVs from the other applicants – except for the one who sent us that rude email!

2 Write TRUE if the statement is true according to the passage.
FALSE if the statement is not true according to the passage.
NOT GIVEN if the statement is not given in the passage.

1 None of the applicants were suitable.   _____
2 It was difficult to narrow down the number of applicants.   _____
3 This website often employs new journalists themselves.   _____
4 The advertiser found the right person for the job.   _____
5 Most of the applicants could do the job.   _____

 Check your answers.

Vocabulary

1 Complete the sentences. Use these words.

> stock broadcasting communication foreign radio
> press electronic computer government news

1 Reuters is a well-known worldwide _____ agency.
2 He works as a DJ at the local _____ station.
3 *ABC* stands for the Australian _____ Corporation.
4 I've seen her on the television! She's the _____ broadcaster for ITV.
5 Podcasts and smart phones are just two examples of the recent advances in _____ technology.
6 Wall Street is the home of the New York _____ exchange.
7 People can now buy and sell stocks and shares on the Internet. This is known as the _____ marketplace.
8 If you visit another country, you will need to buy _____ currency.
9 Britain and Australia have a free press. This means that they can write what they want to, without _____ influence.
10 Facts about viewing figures for TV and radio programmes are stored on the _____ database.

 Check your answers.

Pronunciation acronyms

1 Match the acronyms and abbreviations with the full forms.

1 MSc   A International Standard Book Number
2 IELTS   B Compact Disc Read-Only Memory
3 ISBN   C Bachelor of Arts
4 BA   D International English Language Testing System
5 CD-ROM   E Master of Science

 Check your answers.

🎧 **14** Now listen and practise saying the acronyms and abbreviations.

1 It is important to choose the correct form of a word. Look at the entries for *photograph*. Complete the sentences, choosing the correct form.

1 The _____ took a _____ of the bride and groom standing under the trees.

2 He can always remember new vocabulary – he has a _____ memory.

3 Students who are interested in _____ can join a club at the Students' Union.

photograph /ˈfəʊtəˌɡrɑːf/ (also **photo**) *noun* [C] a picture that is taken with a camera: *to take a photograph*

photographer /fəˈtɒɡrəfə/ *noun* [C] a person who takes photographs

photographic /ˌfəʊtəˈɡræfɪk/ *adj.* connected with photographs or photography

photography /fəˈtɒɡrəfi/ *noun* [U] the skill or process of taking photographs

2 Now look at the entries again and answer the questions.

1 How is the main stress marked in the dictionary?

2 How does the word stress change with the different forms of the word *photograph*?

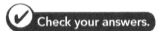

present perfect

1 Complete the sentences with the present perfect tense. Use the words in the brackets.

1 Harold Jakes _____ (work/never/as a sports journalist).

2 _____ Harold Jakes _____ (live/ever/in America)?

3 Harold Jakes _____ (report/BBC/since 1992).

4 Candace Weingold _____ (work/always/America).

5 She _____ (do/some live reporting).

6 She _____ (never/work on a music programme).

7 _____ Candace _____ (take/degree in media journalism)?

8 Both Harold Jakes and Candace _____ (work/media/more than ten years).

9 Neither of them _____ (have/ever/experience as an anchorman).

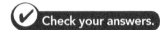

2 Use the words in the box to say what has happened in the pictures.
Use the present perfect tense.

land have find win

1 Doctors _____ finally _____ a cure for the common cold.

2 The Americans _____ on Mars.

3 A woman from Manchester _____ five baby boys.

4 Manchester United _____ the cup!

giving reasons

3 Give reasons for the events in sentences 1–5. Use the different expressions below, and choose a reason from the box.

this is because . . .   this is caused by . . .   this is the effect of . . .

subject + verb clause	noun phrase
they can be produced more cheaply nowadays	cheaper production
they watch too much television	too much television
more people now have broadband	the popularity of broadband
the world is getting warmer	global warming
they had satellite TV first	the earlier introduction of satellite TV

1 The ice at the North Pole is melting.
This is the effect of global warming.
This is because the world is getting warmer.
This is caused by global warming.

2 Cable TV never became popular in Britain.

3 Most people in Britain now have a home computer.

4 The Internet is now a very popular source of news.

5 Children today have poor communication skills.

1 Read the advertisement and

Write   TRUE if the statement is true.
FALSE if the statement is false.
NOT GIVEN if the statement is not given in the passage.

1 The applicant will need to have more than one type of skill.   _____

2 Experience is more important than qualifications for this job.   _____

3 The job involves working inside and outside the studio.   _____

4 The applicant needs to be able to work well with other people.   _____

WHKY Evening Broadcast News Anchorman

Job Description

The successful applicant for this post will be an experienced broadcaster, responsible for general reporting on a variety of assignments: live news, feature reports, interviews and phone-ins. He or she will also produce and contribute to our news magazine, *The WHKY Listener*. The applicant should have excellent speaking ability and a friendly conversational manner. Those who have the relevant qualifications, plus imagination, creativity and energy, should apply for this rewarding position.

Qualifications

Applicants will need at least three years' experience in a relevant field. Radio reporting experience is preferred. Some experience as a radio producer is required. We will also require at least a Bachelor's degree in journalism or media communications; a Master's degree is preferred. The applicant must be able to work in a team, and be familiar with American Public Broadcasting standards.

2 🎧 **15** Listen to a conversation and complete the sentences. Write no more than three words for each answer.

1 The woman thinks that Harold Jakes is _____ for the job.

2 The radio station does not need any more _____ to work there.

3 Mr Jakes probably did some _____ in his job as a presenter.

4 Mr Jakes does not have _____.

5 Candace Weingold's nationality is _____.

6 Ms Weingold has done a lot of _____ reporting.

7 She has worked for a _____ since 2005.

8 She has a Bachelor's degree in _____.

✔ **Check your answers.**

1 Read the advertisement and choose the appropriate word in brackets to complete the letter.

> Location: Central London, Salary: £18,000. Job description: one of Europe's leading production companies based in Soho is seeking an outgoing and friendly receptionist with media experience and a great personality, to start as soon as possible. You will meet and greet clients, answer phones, take care of the post and do day-to-day office work. Send your CV now!

Dear Sir or (Mrs/Madam),

I have (saw/seen) your advertisement (on/at) the Internet for a receptionist, and I am interested (to/in) applying for the job.

I am 22 years (old/age) and live in South London. I have (recently/yet) completed a course in Media Studies at Maidstone College, and achieved a good (pass/past) on the (lesson/course). My tutors say that I have a good personality, and I (make/do) friends easily. I am (hoping/hoped) to become a production assistant in the future, and the careers (counsellor/chancellor) at the college has (advice/advised) me to take an office job (before/first), because this way I can (learn/learning) how a production company is organised.

I hope you will consider my (application/ask). I have enclosed my CV, and you can see that I have some experience of office (work/works) and good computer skills. I am available for interview (for/at) any time.

I look forward to hearing from you.

Yours (truly/sincerely),

Sweehar Wing

2 Write a letter of application for the same job for yourself.

 Check your answers.

Unit 6

Energy

1 Read the passage and write *C* if the advice is for keeping cool in hot countries, or *W* if it is for keeping warm in cold countries.

How to save energy in your home

1 Have modern windows put in. This will cut heat loss through the windows by 50%, and could save you £40 a year. `w`

2 Don't use the oven during the hot part of the day. ☐

3 Keep window coverings closed in the daytime to reduce build-up of heat. `c`

4 Seal gaps in the floor with newspaper. This costs nothing and will stop heat escaping through the floor. ☐

5 In large rooms, heat only the areas that you use. ☐

6 Make sure that hot air can escape from your roof. ☐

7 Look after your heating system. Don't wait until it breaks down, which will usually be in the middle of winter. ☐

8 Heat rises, and much of it may be escaping through the roof. ☐

9 Plant trees around your house for shade. ☐

10 Don't turn the heating up to maximum. Turn it down and wear warm clothing. ☐

Now decide which advice is useful for your country.

Vocabulary

1 Use a verb or a noun from the box to complete the sentences.

> NOUNS: break   handout   deadline   VERBS: hand in   do   show

1 The students had to _____ a report on the Dinorwig power station.

2 The tutor set a _____ one week before the end of term.

3 In their final presentations, the students will _____ slides with diagrams of Electric Mountain.

4 Dona has prepared a written _____ with information about the turbines.

5 Dona went to Wales to _____ field work.

6 After their work is finished, the students can take a _____.

2 Match the words for types of power with the sources of energy.

1	hydroelectric	**A**	below the ground
2	solar	**B**	the sun
3	nuclear	**C**	the air
4	wind power	**D**	water
5	geothermal	**E**	atoms

 Check your answers.

3 Put the jobs into groups.

> research assistant   professor   administrator   receptionist

1 office:

2 academic:

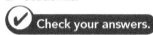 Check your answers.

Listening   IELTS tasks: multiple-choice questions; note completion

1 Match the words with the definitions.

1	eco-friendly	**A**	surrounding area
2	environment	**B**	weather
3	green	**C**	to make dirty
4	to pollute	**D**	working with nature
5	climate	**E**	not wanting to cause damage to nature

 Check your answers.

🎧 **16 Now listen to an interview and circle three letters A–F.**

A BedZED is in south London.

B Felicity Campbell is a teacher.

C The houses in BedZED are all the same.

D There are 82 houses in BedZED.

E Felicity drives a car.

F Some of the houses are cheaper than others.

 Check your answers.

2 🎧 **16 Listen again and complete the notes with no more than three words.**

BioRegional is an environmental **(1)** _____. The solar panels are situated **(2)** _____ of the buildings. The houses at BedZED use **(3)** _____ less power than conventional houses. Felicity's house has three **(4)** _____. The houses have workstations instead of a **(5)** _____. The development has a nursery, a cafe and a **(6)** _____. **(7)** _____ houses are very popular.

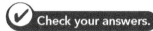 Check your answers.

Language study · present passive

1 Put the words in correct order.

1 into by panels solar turned Sunlight electricity is   *Sunlight is turned into electricity by solar panels.*
2 shared all are residents the Computers by   _____
3 generated 82 heat Enough light is and houses for   _____
4 houses for workers local reserved Some are the of   _____
5 already project planned similar A is   _____
6 most are used Bicycles residents of by the   _____

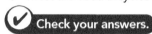 Check your answers.

2 Are these sentences active or passive? Write A for active, P for passive.

1 Wind turbines use the power of the wind to drive a generator.   _____
2 The blades are turned by the movement of the wind.   _____
3 Electricity is generated as the shaft turns the gearbox.   _____
4 The generator uses magnets to convert the energy into electricity.   _____
5 At the next stage, electricity is sent to a transformer nearby.   _____

 Check your answers.

Reading · IELTS tasks: matching headings and paragraphs; true/false/not given

1 Match the definitions with the words.

fission   fusion

1 a reaction in which an atom splits in two, releasing a lot of energy
2 a reaction in which atoms are pushed together to form
   a heavier atom, releasing a lot of energy

 Check your answers.

2 Read the passage and choose the most suitable headings for paragraphs A–F from the list. There are two extra headings.

1 Turning up the heat   _____
2 Effective and clean   _____
3 Hope for the future   _____
4 A safer alternative   _____
5 Gas versus coal   _____
6 The power of nature   _____
7 An early success   _____
8 The story of fission   _____

 Check your answers.

Nuclear Fusion

A Nuclear power is currently produced by fission or splitting of atoms. This method produces dangerous by-products which are difficult to dispose of, and there is the possibility of radioactive fallout as in the Chernobyl disaster of 1986. Fusion, on the other hand, is a relatively safe process which does not rely on dangerous fuels.

B Most people have heard of Einstein's formula, $E = mc^2$, but what does it mean? In fact, it is a description of how mass is converted into energy, and it is this energy which powers the stars, including our own sun. If we can reproduce this process on earth, we will have an infinite source of energy which does not rely on fossil fuels such as coal, gas or oil. One source of fuel for nuclear fusion is deuterium, which is a type of hydrogen found in ordinary water.

C Conventional ways of generating power are wasteful. Typically, 60–90% of the energy generated is lost, meaning that we can only use 10–40%. There is also the problem of waste materials and pollution. Nuclear fusion is more than ten million times more efficient than burning coal as a source of energy.

D The main difficulty in recreating the process of fusion on earth is the enormously high temperature which must be generated. Fusion occurs naturally in the sun, which is at a temperature of ten million K. This temperature must then be maintained long enough for the reaction to take place.

E The first machine to reach the required temperature was the Tokamak, which was developed by Russian scientists in 1968. The Tokamak is a doughnut-shaped chamber surrounded by magnets, which create a strong electric current. The Tokamak could only maintain this temperature for a few milliseconds, but this was the first time it had been achieved. Scientists are now working with lasers to increase the temperature.

F It seems that it may be only a matter of time before we are able to produce enough power for all our needs, from a plentiful source, without causing damage to the planet. If so, imagine the benefits it would bring.

Check your answers.

3 Read the passage again. Do the statements reflect the claims of the writer?

Write   **TRUE** if the statement reflects the claims of the writer.
FALSE if the statement contradicts the claims of the writer.
NOT GIVEN if it is impossible to say what the writer thinks about this.

1 Einstein's formula shows how the sun gets its power. _____

2 Nuclear fusion can use water as a source of fuel. _____

3 Burning coal is an efficient source of energy. _____

4 To achieve fusion, the temperature must be maintained for more than one second. _____

5 The Tokomak is powered by lasers. _____

 **Check your answers.**

4 Now complete the sentences. Use these words.

| by-product | radioactive fallout | fossil fuel | laser |

1 The trees had all died because of the _____ from the nuclear power station.

2 A _____ is something that is made while making something else.

3 The surgeon used a _____ to perform the delicate eye operation.

4 Coal is an example of a _____.

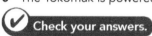 **Check your answers.**

1 Read the sentences and find 12 words about energy in your dictionary. The words can go in any direction: ↓, →, ←, ↙, or ↘.

1 f_____ and f_____ are two ways of making atomic energy.

2 To operate our lights and computers, we need to use e_____ p_____.

3 Heat comes from the earth's centre. This is called g_____ energy.

4 A t_____ is a large machine which is used to g_____ electricity.

5 The movement of electricity is called a c_____.

6 Coal, gas and oil are all types of fossil f_____. Burning these can p_____ the environment.

7 A d_____ is used to contain water, but a p_____ is used to move it upwards.

✔ **Check your answers.**

P	E	T	G	E	N	E	R	A	T	E	F
A	P	P	U	G	L	A	T	Y	R	L	G
H	U	O	T	N	E	R	R	U	C	E	H
T	M	D	W	I	F	W	U	G	O	C	E
U	P	W	P	E	E	G	K	T	L	T	S
R	K	B	A	L	R	N	H	O	F	R	P
B	P	K	H	D	Y	E	F	R	I	I	N
I	F	R	R	R	I	W	C	S	C	R
N	U	D	A	M	V	N	O	I	S	U	F
E	D	E	A	I	S	L	A	B	I	Z	U
L	R	L	P	E	T	U	L	L	O	P	E
R	Y	L	G	W	A	M	D	P	N	M	L

1 Put the words into groups, according to the sound of the underlined letters.

pollute   report   workstation   do   turbine   current   fuel   pump
transformer   hub   combustion   geothermal   nuclear

1 ɜː her   _____
2 ɔː more   _____
3 ʌ but   _____
4 uː food   _____

 17 Now listen and check your answers.

✔ **Check your answers.**

2 17 Listen again and practise.

1 Divide the paragraph into five sentences, using full stops (.) and CAPITAL LETTERS.

> second, the intake, where gates on the dam are opened and water is pulled through the penstock – a pipe that leads to the turbine water pressure is built up as it flows through this pipe third, and perhaps the most important component, is the turbine the turbine houses large blades, which are hit by the water and are attached to a generator above it through a drive shaft the most common type of turbine for hydropower plants is the Francis Turbine, which looks like a big disc with curved blades

 Check your answers.

2 Complete the passage. Use these words and phrases once only.

| at the next stage | by | so that | so as to | firstly | finally | in order to |

SOLAR SPACE HEATING

Many large buildings which are used for storing goods need clean air and controlled temperatures. This can be expensive, because it uses a lot of energy. **(1)** _____ save costs, some companies are now using a solar ventilation system. **(2)** _____, a thin sheet of metal is fixed to a south-facing wall **(3)** _____ collect heat from the sun.

(4) _____ air passes through small holes in the metal panel. A space is left between the wall of the building and the metal panel **(5)** _____, the air streams can mix together. **(6)** _____ the hot air is sucked into the building **(7)** _____ a fan. This fan is the only moving part in the whole process.

 Check your answers.

Now label the diagram. Use these words.

outside air
metal panel with holes
building wall
hot air
fan

 Check your answers.

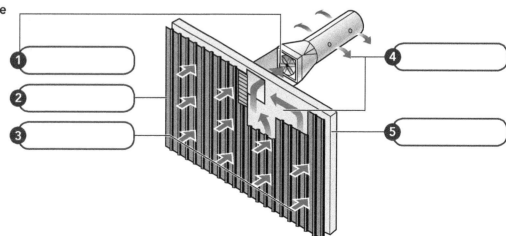

Unit 7

Cities

Vocabulary

1 Complete the passage. Use these words.

terrible   pleasant   overcrowded   modern   humid   dynamic   dirty   coastal

MUMBAI

Mumbai can be a fascinating city to spend time in. Whether you find the experience **(1)** _____ and enjoyable, however, will depend largely on how well you can deal with the heat, the **(2)** _____, wet climate, the **(3)** _____ traffic fumes and the **(4)** _____ poverty of India's busiest city. Mumbai suffers from a serious lack of space. In fact, it could well be the most **(5)** _____ city in the world. In less than five hundred years, it has grown from a small, **(6)** _____ fishing area into a megalopolis of 21 million people. The roots of the population problem lie, surprisingly, in the city's ability to create wealth. Mumbai handles half the country's foreign trade and its movie industry is the biggest in the world. Symbols of wealth are everywhere; from the **(7)** _____ new office blocks situated on Nariman Point, to the **(8)** _____ and cosmopolitan atmosphere of the Colaba district, famous for its night clubs.

 Check your answers.

Language study   comparatives and superlatives

1 Complete the passage using the comparative form of the adjectives in brackets.

Getting around Sydney

Driving can be problematic for the visitor in central Sydney, so it is **(1)** _____ (easy) and **(2)** _____ (good) to take a taxi instead. Although it is **(3)** _____ (expensive) compared with public transport, it is **(4)** _____ (fast) and **(5)** _____ (pleasant).

Now continue to complete the passage using the correct superlative form of the adjectives in brackets.

The buses and ferries of Sydney provide some of the **(1)** _____ (cheap) and **(2)** _____ (pleasant) sightseeing opportunities in Australia. A ferry trip to Manly passes some beautiful harbour sites, while a bus trip to Vaucluse offers some of the **(3)** _____ (good) views. Sydney's rail network is extensive. The underground city centre train loop is the **(4)** _____ (fast) way of getting around, but unfortunately does not offer the **(5)** _____ (beautiful) or interesting views.

Reading IELTS tasks: multiple choice questions; summarising

1 Read the passage quickly and choose the correct answer A–D.

1 The text is taken from a/an . . .

   A atlas   B prospectus   C article   D journal

Now complete the table. Use no more than three words for each point.

Change	Result
Urban sprawl	affects **(1)** _____
	leads to higher **(2)** _____
	increase in demand for **(3)** _____
	loss of **(4)** _____

World's biggest cities merging into 'mega-regions'

The world's megacities, defined as cities with populations of over 10 million, are merging to form vast 'mega-regions' which may stretch hundreds of kilometres across countries and be home to more than 100 million people, according to a United Nations report.

The 'endless city' could be one of the most significant developments – and problems – in the way people live and economies grow in the next 50 years. The largest of these is the China mega-region, home to about 120 million people in the area around Hong Kong, Shenhzen and Guangzhou. Other mega-regions have formed in Japan and Brazil. More than 43 million people in the South America mega-region live in Rio de Janeiro and Sao Paulo in Brazil and the area in between. Similar regions are developing in India and West Africa. Urbanisation is now 'unstoppable' with just over 50% of the world's people now living in cities. By 2050, over 70% of the world population will be urban dwellers. By then, only 14% of people in rich countries will live outside cities and 33% in poor countries.

The development of mega-regions is regarded as generally positive as they, rather than countries, are now driving wealth. Research shows that the world's largest 40 mega-regions cover only a tiny fraction of the habitable surface of the planet and are home to fewer than 18% of the world's population. However, they account for 66% of all economic activity and about 85% of technological and scientific innovation. The top 25 cities in the world account for more than half the world's wealth and the five largest cities in India and China now account for 50% of those countries' wealth.

However, the growth of mega-regions is also leading to 'urban sprawl' as they spread out into the countryside in an unplanned way. Cities like Los Angeles grew 45% in numbers between 1975 and 1990 but tripled their surface area over the same period. Urban sprawl is wasteful as it impacts on transport costs, increases energy consumption, requires more resources and reduces areas of farmland. The more unequal cities become, the higher the risk that economic differences will result in social and political tension. The cities that are prospering the most are generally those that are reducing inequalities.

2 Complete the summary. Use some of these words.

70%   a small part   a large proportion   economically   growth   increases   marginally   migration
differences   more than half   most   over ten million   poverty   society   the majority

The growth of urban areas is going to be one of the most significant factors affecting **(1)** _____
over the next fifty years. **(2)** _____ of the world's population currently lives in cities. Megacities –
cities with **(3)** _____ inhabitants – are connecting with other cities to form mega-regions which
are linked physically and **(4)** _____. The world's 40 biggest mega-regions cover
(5) _____ of the habitable surface of earth. Although large urban areas can enjoy rapid
(6) _____ they also face **(7)** _____ in social and political tension as a result of
economic **(8)** _____.

✓ Check your answers.

Listening   IELTS tasks: multiple-choice questions; note completion

1 🎧 18 Listen and choose the correct answer A–C.

1 The theme of the talk is personal safety . . .
   A on campus.
   B on public transport.
   C on the streets.

2 The speaker says personal attack alarms . . .
   A are always effective.
   B should be carried by hand.
   C are available in all DIY shops.

3 Personal attack alarms cost approximately . . . pounds.
   A two
   B five
   C ten

4 Cyclists and joggers are not recommended to use . . .
   A main paths.
   B open spaces.
   C wooded areas.

✓ Check your answers.

2 🎧 18 Listen again and complete the notes using no more than three words for each answer.

When walking . . .
Keep to (1) _____ areas.
Don't take short cuts through parks or (2) _____ .
Try to walk (3) _____ .
Buy a personal attack alarm which will work when (4) _____ .
Carry your bag (5) _____ .
When cycling and jogging . . . Try to change your (6) _____ on a regular basis.
Avoid wearing MP3 player headphones so that you can (7) _____ or someone
approaching (8) _____ .

✓ Check your answers.

3 Now choose the correct letter A–C.

1 A Keys ☐   B Personal attack alarm ☐   C MP3 player ☐
   . . . should be kept in your hand to increase personal safety.

2 Which means of transport is NOT mentioned in the talk?
   A taxi ☐   B bus ☐   C car ☐

3 The main purpose of the talk is to . . .
   A persuade. ☐   B advise. ☐   C warn. ☐

✓ Check your answers.

Pronunciation | weak forms in comparatives

1 🎧 **19** Listen and write down the number of words you hear; *it's* = two words.

 Check your answers.

2 🎧 **20** When words are spoken together, many weak vowels are pronounced /ə/. Listen and underline the sound /ə/ in the phrases.

1 much better to be	**5** it's better to
2 in some larger	**6** far more important than
3 no more than	**7** you can be seen more easily
4 will be less than	**8** much safer to

 Check your answers.

3 🎧 **20** Listen and practise saying the phrases.

 Check your answers.

Writing | IELTS tasks: classifying; comparing charts

1 Look at the chart and answer the questions.

1 What does the chart show?
2 What percentage of young people and older people go to fast food restaurants?
3 What percentage of young people and older people go to night clubs?

 Check your answers.

Leisure activities in British cities by age

activity	16–24 years	25–34 years	35–44 years	45–59 years	60 years +
meal in a restaurant (not fast food)	63%	69%	65%	75%	70%
meal in a fast food restaurant	77%	74%	55%	34%	11%
cinema	65%	51%	31%	23%	11%
sports events	31%	34%	36%	22%	11%
visit historic building	24%	30%	35%	39%	30%
disco or night club	68%	47%	20%	9%	3%
museum or art gallery	21%	18%	27%	26%	19%
pub or bar	82%	85%	81%	74%	55%
theatre	14%	18%	15%	18%	17%

2 Put the sentences into groups.

1 comparing   **2** contrasting   **3** classifying

1 We can divide the leisure activities into several groups.
2 It is clear that enjoyment of fast food decreases as people get older. A teenager is seven times more likely to spend time in a fast food restaurant in contrast with an older person.
3 For example, we can make a distinction between indoor leisure activities such as theatre, pubs and restaurants and outdoor interests such as visits to historic buildings.
4 Similarly, the same pattern is reflected in visits to the cinema. You are much less likely to see an older person at a film in contrast with someone in their early twenties.
5 However, all age groups have in common a similar attitude to the theatre. Just as many young people as old spend time there.
6 Likewise, you can expect to find as many young people as old people in museums and art galleries.

 Check your answers.

Study skills   grouping

1 It is a good idea to put words and phrases into groups to help you remember them. Put the phrases in the table.

to make a distinction between ... and ...	in the same way
to have in common	in comparison with ...
to divide the information into	however ...
in contrast with	compared with
similarly	as ... as
likewise	

Classifying	Contrasting	Comparing

 Check your answers.

Now describe the chart in Writing 1. Write 150 words.

Communication

Vocabulary

1 Match the text messages with the meanings.

text message		meaning	
1	CUL8R	A	thanks
2	THX	B	bye for now
3	MTNG	C	see you later
4	XLNT	D	free to talk?
5	RU	E	meeting
6	B4N	F	excellent
7	F2T?	G	are you

 Check your answers.

2 Complete the passage. Use these words.

prizes   keypad   premium rate   key word   screen   call   information   cost   charged   key

WHAT IS SMS?

SMS, or short message service, is great for sending quick little messages to friends' phones and usually cheaper than a mobile phone **(1)** _____. You simply key the message in and the recipient reads it on the **(2)** _____. So, next time you're late you can just key in *CUL8R*. In older mobile phones you write the letters by pressing the key repeatedly on a numeric **(3)** _____. So, if you press the **(4)** _____ 2 once, it writes an 'A', if you press it twice, a 'B' and three times a 'C'. In recent times many publishers and games companies have started to introduce special services which provide **(5)** _____ such as the latest world news or sports results. You can receive such a service by dialling a **(6)** _____ telephone number to cover the **(7)** _____ to the company of sending you the messages. Or, by sending a simple text message to a mobile number with a **(8)** _____ such as 'START'. If you have not paid for the messages as part of the registration you will probably be **(9)** _____ for each text alert message you receive. So, always read the service details carefully. Nothing in this world is free and there are no **(10)** _____ for knowing that.

 Check your answers.

1 Read the passage. Do the statements agree with the information given in the reading passage?

Write TRUE if the statement is true according to the passage.
FALSE if the statement is false according to the passage.
NOT GIVEN if the statement is not given in the passage.

1 A lot of research has been done on yawning. _____
2 An average yawn lasts less than ten seconds. _____
3 Yawning happens when people are sad. _____
4 The yawning reflex starts after birth. _____
5 People who do exercise appear to yawn more than people who do not. _____
6 Jaw and face muscles are used during the yawning reflex. _____

✓ Check your answers.

Yawning

People communicate in many different ways and yawning is one important means of non-verbal communication. It gives many different messages to people, and everyone yawns. Some birds, reptiles, fish and most mammals also yawn. However, the reason why we do it is still a mystery. There is also very little research available on yawning as for most people, it is not a problematic reflex. Here are a few things that are known about yawns:

1 The average duration of a yawn is about six seconds.
2 In humans, the earliest yawn happens about eleven weeks after conception.
3 Yawns become contagious to people between the first and second years of life.

Many people assume we yawn because our bodies are trying to get rid of extra carbon dioxide and to take in more oxygen. This may make some sense. According to this theory, when people are bored or tired, they breathe more slowly. As breathing slows down, less oxygen gets to the lungs. As carbon dioxide builds up in the blood, a message to the brain results in signals back to the lungs saying 'Take a deep breath', and a yawn is produced.

The only problem with this theory is that it may not be true. In 1987, Dr Provine, a professor of Psychology and Neuroscience at the University of Maryland, set up an experiment to test the theory that high carbon dioxide/low oxygen blood content causes yawning. Neither carbon dioxide gas or oxygen caused the students to yawn more. These gases also did not change the duration of the yawns when they occurred.

The researchers also looked for a relationship between breathing and yawning by having people exercise. Exercise, obviously, causes people to breathe faster. However, the number of yawns during exercise was not different from the number of yawns before or after exercise. Therefore, it appears that yawning is not due to carbon dioxide/oxygen levels in the blood and that yawning and breathing are controlled by different mechanisms.

So, the question remains – why do we yawn? Dr Provine suggests that perhaps yawning is like stretching. Yawning and stretching increase blood pressure and heart rate. Evidence that yawning or stretching may be related comes from the observation that if you try to stop a yawn by keeping your mouth shut, the yawn is not satisfying. For some reason, the stretching of jaw and face muscles is necessary for a good yawn.

According to Provine, it is possible that yawns are contagious because at one time in history, the yawn coordinated the social behaviour of a group of animals. When one member of the group yawned, all the other members of the group also yawned. Yawns may still be contagious these days because of a response that is not used any more. None of this has been proven true and yawns are still one of the mysteries of the mind.

2 Complete the summary using one or two words from the reading passage for each answer.

Yawning is a reflex characterised by the **(1)** _____ of muscles of the jaw and the face. For years, scientists believed that yawning was a response to lower levels of **(2)** _____. However, Provine sees yawning as a **(3)** _____ signal. His theory is that group yawning is a **(4)** _____ from the time we were tribal creatures. Although no one knows for certain why, yawning is certainly a behaviour that is **(5)** _____.

✓ Check your answers.

1 🎧 **21** **Listen to an interview and choose the correct letter A–C.**

1 Mobile phones are stolen in one . . . of all cases of street theft.
  A third
  B quarter
  C half

2 Roz Thorpe is a . . .
  A local councillor.
  B crime prevention officer.
  C police inspector.

3 Your IMEI number can be located by pressing . . .
  A *##016.
  B #*06#.
  C *#06#.

4 You should mark your phone with your . . .
  A name and postcode.
  B name and house number.
  C postcode and house number.

5 You can get a marking kit . . .
  A at some department stores.
  B online.
  C from police stations.

6 Marking kits cost . . . pounds.
  A two
  B five
  C ten

7 It is NOT a good idea to keep your phone . . . when on the street.
  A in a bag
  B in your hand
  C in your pocket

8 The campaign is using . . . to raise awareness of mobile phone theft.
  A posters
  B leaflets
  C television campaigns

🎧 **21** **Now listen again and complete the notes using no more than three words for each answer.**

Mobile Phone Precautions

- Record the IMEI number – (this is **(1)** _____ to each phone).
- Property mark your phone with your **(2)** _____ and house number (for example **(3)** _____).
- Always keep it **(4)** _____ in public places.
- **(5)** _____ when not needed.
- In the event of loss or theft **(6)** _____.

✓ Check your answers.

2 Complete the information using no more than one word for each answer.

MOBILE PHONE THEFT

Protect your phone!
Lock it!
(1) _____ it!
Keep it!
(2) _____ it!
Don't (3) _____ it!

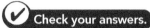
Check your answers.

Language study real conditionals; *in case, unless*

1 Match the beginnings with the ends of each sentence.

1 If you take a few practical steps . . .   **A** you can buy a marking kit.
2 If your phone goes missing . . .   **B** switch it off.
3 If you go to a DIY shop . . .   **C** you can't go wrong.
4 If you don't need to use your phone . . .   **D** report it to the police.

Check your answers.

2 Complete the sentences. Use these words and phrases.

| if   unless   in case of   in case |

1 Write down your identification number _____ your phone is stolen.
2 _____ your phone goes missing, the police can use this special number to identify it.
3 You can find out your phone's unique number _____ you press star-hash-zero-six-hash.
4 Property marking your phone provides you with even more protection _____ theft or loss.
5 _____ you go to your local DIY store, you can buy a marking kit for a couple of pounds.
6 Try to keep your phone out of sight _____ you are out and about.
7 _____ you actually need to use your phone, keep it turned off.
8 Make sure you report it missing immediately _____ it is lost or stolen.
9 Lock it, mark it and keep it _____ you lose it.

Check your answers.

Pronunciation real conditionals

1 🎧 **22** Listen and notice the pronunciation. Mark how the voice rises and falls.

1 If you take a few practical steps, you can't go wrong.
2 If your phone goes missing, the police can identify it.
3 If you press star-hash-zero-six-hash, you can find out your phone's unique number.
4 Try to keep your phone out of sight if you are walking on the street.

🎧 **22** Now listen again and practice.

Writing · IELTS tasks: essay planning

1 Read the essay title and underline the key words.

> What are the advantages and disadvantages of having a mobile phone?
> *You should write at least 250 words.*

Check your answers.

Now add more notes and examples to the plan.

Advantages	Examples
Easy to communicate with people _____	_____
_____	_____

Disadvantages	Examples
Health risks _____	_____
_____	_____

2 Complete the essay with the examples and supporting information.

A both to buy and maintain.

B I can now reach him at any time in any location.

C in the past when I called my partner in Afghanistan, most of the time he wasn't in the city or he was in places where he had no access to a telephone.

D it has virtually become a necessity for people everywhere

E it makes our lives easier and more convenient.

F it was not portable so you could only contact friends or colleagues when they were at home or in the office

G Mobile phones have made it very simple to get in touch with people even when they are in very remote parts of the world.

H tiredness, headaches and loss of concentration.

I When we use a mobile phone in a public place someone may be listening to us.

Check your answers.

Now decide how many of your advantages and disadvantages from your notes were included in the essay.

3 Write your own essay, using your notes in the table in activity 1.

Nowadays the mobile phone forms an important part of our everyday lives. In fact (1) _____D_____ . Indeed, if we go back twenty years or so, it used to be very difficult to reach somebody by means of the traditional phone when you needed to. This was because (2) _____ . Since the arrival of mobile phones, this problem has disappeared altogether.

The main benefit of mobile phones is that they enable us to make contact much faster and more efficiently. (3) _____ . For example, (4) _____ . By using my mobile phone, (5) _____ . However there are some drawbacks connected with mobile phones. They have been linked to health problems such as (6) _____ . A further disadvantage is the lack of privacy. (7) _____ . Finally, mobile phones can be costly (8) _____ .

On balance, however, I feel that the advantages of owning a mobile phone outweigh the disadvantages. It is a necessity for modern day living because (9) _____ .

1 Here is a list of services and resources that you can find in a library or resource centre. Try to identify them.

1 eeeefrnce koosb _reference books_
2 nedlngi eecsrvi _____
3 alorpssefion slnaourj _____
4 spapewensr _____
5 seamzagin _____
6 tteinern _____
7 VDD yaperl _____
8 idailgt scersuro _____

 Check your answers.

2 Answer the questions.

1 Which of the things in activity 1 do you use already?

_____

2 Which would you like to try in future?

_____

Unit 9

Fitness and health

1 Match the words with pictures 1–8.

| fencing football handball lacrosse cricket basketball rowing sailing |

 1 ____

 2 ____

 3 ____

 4 ____

 5 ____

 6 ____

 7 ____

 8 ____

2 Read the text and answer the questions.

Open Day at the Sports Centre

Get fit with a free one-day trial at the Sports Centre.

10 – 11 **Yoga** – improve your flexibility with stretching and bending activities.

11 – 12 **Juggling** – eye and hand co-ordination, are you quick enough?

12 – 1 **Jogging, walking and rowing** – get on the treadmills and rowing machines, improve your muscular endurance.

1 – 3 **Body building** – weights for the arms, leg curl bench for the legs, and pec deck for the chest: get in shape with a body building session.

1 What do you do in yoga?

2 Which activities improve your endurance?

3 How can you improve your muscular strength?

Pictures, diagrams and illustrations are a good way of organising vocabulary learning.
Draw your own pictures or use photos from magazines. Match A–L in the picture with 1–12.

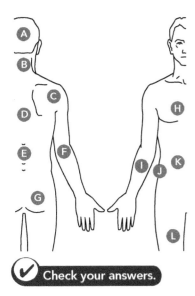

1	head	_____
2	stomach	_____
3	bottom	_____
4	chest	_____
5	neck	_____
6	arm	_____
7	elbow	_____
8	back	_____
9	leg	_____
10	hips	_____
11	shoulder	_____
12	spine	_____

✔ Check your answers.

Reading IELTS tasks: matching headings with paragraphs; true/false/not given

1 Do the quiz.

1 People are becoming less active because . . .
   A of domestic machines. ☐
   B they eat too much. ☐
   C of domestic machines and television. ☐

2 We can measure how hard a person is working in . . . ways.
   A one ☐
   B two ☐
   C three ☐

3 To be healthy, people need to be active for . . .
   A 30 minutes, three days a week. ☐
   B five minutes, five days a week. ☐
   C 30 minutes, five days a week. ☐

Now read the passage on page 59 quickly and check your answers.

2 Read the passage again and match the headings with the paragraphs.

1 Intensity   2 Frequency   3 Duration   4 Expert advice   5 Moving pictures

✔ Check your answers.

The no-motion society

A We are increasingly living in a world where physical activity is taken out of our lives. We have domestic appliances to wash and dry for us, cars to transport us and desks to sit at and work or study. One of the first lessons we learn at school is to *sit still* – and we see nothing unusual in spending hours sitting or lying down while pictures move on a box in front of us.

B This relates to how many times a week you need to exercise in order to become fitter or improve your health. To be healthy, experts recommend being physically active on at least five days out of seven.

C Physical activity can be measured in a number of different ways. In a laboratory it can be measured through looking at how much oxygen a person is taking into the body and delivering to the working muscles. In the gym it can be measured using a heart rate monitor, which records the heart rate at different workloads. The intensity at which you work can be described as either strenuous, moderate or mild. What constitutes a strenuous, moderate or mild exercise workload for you will depend on your current state of health and fitness. Mild to moderate levels of

physical activity are all that's required to keep us fit. For many of us, this means walking quickly. Again, this depends on your current state of health or fitness.

D This is the length of time you need to spend being physically active in any one session. According to much of the research conducted over the past 20 years, you need to be active for up to 30 minutes, five days a week in order to benefit your health. If you haven't done much activity for some time, it's important to build up to this level over a period of weeks. This might mean starting with a walk of just five minutes.

E The recommended physical activity guidelines from experts suggest that to improve your health you should build up to being physically active at a moderate intensity for 30 minutes, five days a week. A little goes a long way. The key message is that any physical activity, no matter how small, is better than none. With the huge social and cultural influences that stop us from moving, any physical activity is a health gain. There is no magic amount of exercise you need to do to get a benefit, the key is to make an effort and persevere. As soon as you move, you win!

3 Do the statements agree with the information given in the reading passage?

Write   TRUE if the statement is true according to the passage.
              FALSE if the statement is false according to the passage.
              NOT GIVEN if the statement is not given in the passage.

1 Household machines mean we are less active at home.   _____

2 Intensity is described as how serious a person is.   _____

3 How strenuous an activity is depends on the person.   _____

4 You need to be active for half an hour a week to be fit.   _____

5 There are big social and cultural influences which make us take exercise.   _____

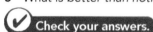 Check your answers.

Now read the passage again and answer the questions.

1 What are the two ways to measure activity intensity?

2 What should people do if they have not done much exercise?

3 What is *better than nothing*?

Check your answers.

Language study   *should(n't), must(n't)*; possibility and certainty

should (n't), must (n't)

1 Complete the passage with *should* or *should not (shouldn't)*.

The Sports Centre

advice for new members

- When you get changed, you **(1)** _____ put your clothes in a locker.

- You **(2)** _____ leave them in the changing room.

- If you are not sure how to use the equipment, you **(3)** _____ ask a member of staff.

- You **(4)** _____ do warm-up exercises before you use the machines – you **(5)** _____ begin exercising immediately.

 Check your answers.

2 Complete the passage with *must* or *must not (mustn't)* and the words in brackets.

> ## The Sports Centre
> ### rules for members
> 1 Only sports centre members are allowed into the sports centre. Students _____
>   (be a member).
> 2 Students are not allowed to use the equipment before they are given training by an instructor. Students
>   _____ (have/training session).
> 3 The Sports Centre is a non-smoking area. Members _____ (smoke).
> 4 The gym is a quiet area – MP3 players are not allowed. Members _____
>   (use MP3 players).

 Check your answers.

3 Look at the pictures and write two pieces of advice with *should* or *shouldn't* for the person in each picture.

1 _____   2 _____   3 _____

   _____   _____   _____

possibility and certainty: *will, might, may*

4 Complete the conversation. Use *will, can, might* or *may*. In some places more than one answer is possible.

Paul: How many players do you think we'll get for next week's five-a-side football match, Ahmed?

Ahmed: I don't know. Steve really wants to play, he **(1)** _____ definitely come.

Paul: OK, that's great. What about Li Feng?

Ahmed: I'm not sure about him, it depends on whether or not he can finish his essay. He **(2)** _____ play.

Paul: I see. How about Hamed?

Ahmed: He'll probably play. He's really busy but he **(3)** _____ come if I help him with an assignment.

Paul: So that's one definite and two possible players.

Ahmed: There is one other person who **(4)** _____ definitely play.

Paul: Who's that?

Ahmed: Carmen – she **(5)** _____ be able to play, she's free on that day.

Paul: OK – tell her she's on the team.

 Check your answers.

5 Complete the diagram. Use these words.

probably   likely to be   certain to be   possibly

100%	75%	60%	50%	0%

 Check your answers.

Now complete the passage.

Tao: Who do you think will win the European Cup this year?
Sara: Well, Manchester United are really playing well, they **(1)** _____ to be in the final. What do you think?
Tao: Manchester United won't win, Barcelona are much better, they **(2)** _____ the winners.
Catherine: I don't know – Galatasaray are really improving, I think they have a good chance, they could **(3)** _____ get to the final. What about your team, Istvan?
Istvan: Ferencváros? I don't think they'll win, they'll **(4)** _____ go out in the fourth round.

 Check your answers.

6 Complete the sentences with *can* or *could*. In some places there is more than one answer.

LONG-DISTANCE RUNNING

When you are long-distance running, here are some things to do and some things to avoid:

1 Build up your distance little by little: do three miles in the first week, five in the second and so on. Don't run long distances immediately, you _____ _____ (hurt yourself).

2 When you are running, drink plenty of water; runners that don't drink water _____ _____ (suffer/dehydration).

3 Make sure you have a good pair of running shoes; with bad shoes you _____ (hurt/knees and feet).

4 If you are in pain, you should stop running or you _____ (make/worse).

 Check your answers.

Pronunciation   *should(n't), must(n't)*

1 🎧 **23** Listen to the recording and practise the pronunciation of *should*, *shouldn't*, *must* and *mustn't*. Pay attention to the final sound.

🎧 **23** Now listen again and practise.

1 🎧 **24** Listen to the yoga instructor and put the pictures in order.

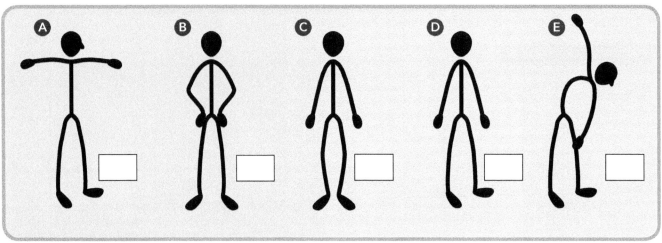

✓ Check your answers.

2 🎧 **25** Listen to a talk about lacrosse and match the times with the events.

1 centuries ago   A Lacrosse became an Olympic sport.
2 17th century   B Europeans first saw the game.
3 1904   C It was played by American Indians.

✓ Check your answers.

3 🎧 **25** Listen again and choose A–C.

1 A Lacrosse is the national sport of North America.
   B The origins of lacrosse are unknown.
   C Lacrosse is the fastest game in the world.

2 A Early games stopped when the sun went down.
   B The number of players in original lacrosse games was limitless.
   C There were many rules in the original game.

3 A The French first saw Choctaw Indians playing the game.
   B Europeans started playing 50 years after they first saw the game.
   C Lacrosse was probably named after a cross used by French bishops.

✓ Check your answers.

Now answer the questions.

1 What were the purposes of the original game?
2 Why were players often injured in the original game?
3 In which country is lacrosse the national sport?

✓ Check your answers.

1 Read the writing task and write three ideas you could include.

> In today's society, many everyday tasks are done by machines and appliances. Do you think this is a positive or negative development?

Now read the essay and see which of your ideas are included.

In the last century, many people did things by hand, but nowadays more and more tasks have become automated.

- Many people have washing machines, clothes driers and dishwashers.
- The amount of activity needed to wash and dry clothes and wash dishes is greatly reduced. As technology progresses, more and more of these tasks will be automatic.
- Vacuum cleaning or cutting the grass.
- Improvements in technology have given us 24-hour a day entertainment from digital TV to video games. This means that there are fewer tasks to do, more time for leisure and more time to be entertained and not do very much.

I think there are at least two positive effects of this.

- We do not need to do repetitive and uninteresting jobs like washing-up and this gives us more time to do other things. What we do with this time depends upon the individual.
- For people who are less able to do these jobs, like elderly or disabled people, these machines are a great help. Future developments may be able to help them even more.

I think that this is the most positive side of technology.

Now I will look at the disadvantages.

- It is up to the individual what they do with this extra time.
- Instead of doing everyday tasks people tend to watch television or play video games.
- Television companies encourage us to watch as much TV as possible. This can lead to an inactive lifestyle and people becoming overweight and unhealthy.

In conclusion, the positive side is that because machines and automation do the things we do not like doing, we gain more time to do other things.

- People who cannot do certain things are able to do them with the help of technology.
- On the negative side we lose the daily activity involved in washing-up, vacuum cleaning and so on, and for some people, this may be the only kind of activity they do.

The danger is that we do not replace these activities with others.

2 Read the essay again and underline the main points.

Now divide the essay into four paragraphs.

3 Replace the bullet points. Use these words and phrases.

> secondly   for example (×2)   so   in addition (×2)   first of all   as I mentioned   unfortunately

Now write the essay in full with paragraphs and linking words.

 Check your answers.

Unit 10

Charities

Vocabulary

1 **Read the statements and match them with the charities.**

1 A 24/7 lifesaving service, whatever the weather.
Please help us save lives at sea.

2 Over one million children in the UK suffer from bad housing.
Children need a home to keep warm and stay healthy.

3 We believe in children, no matter who they are, what they have done or what they have been through.
We will support them, stand up for them and bring out the best in each and every child.

4 Give water. Give life. Give two pounds a month.

Believe in children
Barnardo's — Ⓐ

Shelter — Ⓑ

WaterAid — Ⓒ

R N L I
Lifeboats — Ⓓ

✓ Check your answers.

2 Match the words with the definitions.

| campaign | volunteer | donation | fund | poverty | support | contribute | charity |

1 To give money which goes towards a particular purpose.
2 A sum of money which is collected for a particular purpose.
3 Money given by someone who doesn't want anything in exchange.
4 A person who helps other people without being paid to do it.
5 To help someone.
6 The condition of being very poor.
7 A planned group of activities which are intended to achieve a particular purpose.
8 An organisation which provides money or help for people who are in need.

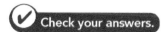 Check your answers.

Now complete the words.

What we do

Oxfam is a **(1)** d_v_l_p_e_t and campaigning organisation. Today, there are millions of people living in **(2)** p_v_r_y across the world. For example, in many villages of western Rajasthan, women do not have the opportunity to go to school or earn an income – Oxfam **(3)** f_n_s local groups that help women to learn new skills and earn money for themselves and their families.

Join Us

Here are just a few of the ways in which you can help Oxfam to achieve its aims:

Make a **(4)** d_n_t_o_. Two pounds a month can help Oxfam change lives. Call us today and **(5)** c_n_r_b_t_ what you can.

Give Time

Oxfam shops need you! Every week more than 22,000 **(6)** v_l_n_e_r_ give 110,000 hours of their time to work in more than 700 Oxfam shops.

Your help and **(7)** s_p_o_t really can make the difference between life and death.

Oxfam is a registered **(8)** c_a_i_y.

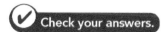 Check your answers.

1 Choose the most suitable headings for paragraphs A–E from the list of headings. There are two extra headings.

List of headings

1 How flexible is voluntary work? ____

2 Can I stop doing voluntary work if I want to? ____

3 What is voluntary work? ____

4 Why do people do voluntary work? ____

5 How can I find out more about voluntary work? ____

6 What are the benefits of voluntary work? ____

7 Are special skills needed for voluntary work? ____

Question and answer: how to become a volunteer

As volunteering week starts we explain what you need to know to get involved . . .

A Voluntary work is working without payment, for a not-for-profit organisation, such as a charity or local community groups. There are thousands of organisations in the UK currently looking for volunteers.

B A lot of people volunteer because they want to give something back to society or make a contribution to their community, often helping out with causes they believe in. As one volunteers' organisation says, *Voluntary work can give people the chance to travel, meet new people and gain new skills*.

C You can volunteer for almost everything. You can give as much or as little of your time as you like, so volunteering is very flexible. However, you will have to agree with the organisation how much time you can give. It could be for one hour a week – or it could be a long-term, full-time commitment, such as a two-year overseas job through Voluntary Service Overseas. You can do volunteer work during the day, the night or at weekends. You can even be a virtual volunteer and do research over the Internet or build a website.

D There are no obligations for you to continue if you are not enjoying the work or feel unhappy – although volunteering organisations advise that you talk first to the organisation you are working for.

E There are several bodies that match volunteers with voluntary organisations, including the National Volunteering Centre. There are also search engines such as the one on the Do-it website that finds volunteering opportunities within a ten-kilometre area of your address.

✓ **Check your answers.**

Now write . . .

1 four advantages of voluntary work. _____

2 two responsibilities of virtual volunteers. _____

3 two sources of information on voluntary work. _____

✓ **Check your answers.**

2 Complete the summary. Choose no more than three words from the passage for each answer.

Volunteers are people who work for charitable organisations on an unpaid basis or to **(1)** _____.
Volunteering provides them with the opportunity to **(2)** _____, to socialise and to learn
(3) _____. Volunteers have control over the amount of **(4)** _____ they give,
ranging from part-time to **(5)** _____ work. Some volunteers even choose to work abroad with
organisations such as **(6)** _____. The **(7)** _____ website contains information about
different volunteering opportunities available locally.

✓ **Check your answers.**

Listening · IELTS tasks: multiple-choice questions; table completion

1 🎧 **26** **Listen to a talk and choose answers A–C.**

1 There are . . . million volunteers in Britain.
A 2   **B** 12   **C** 22

2 The government wants more . . . to do voluntary work.
A teenagers   **B** students   **C** older people

3 Ayesha is a volunteer in a . . .
A library.   **B** bookshop.   **C** school.

4 There are . . . Oxfam shops in the town.
A two   **B** three   **C** five

5 Michael provides transport for elderly people to . . . centres.
A health   **B** community   **C** shopping

6 Michael used to be employed as a . . .
A librarian.   **B** police officer.   **C** taxi driver.

7 Ayesha found a rare book which sold for . . . pounds.
A 16   **B** 60   **C** 600

8 Ayesha has developed . . . skills.
A writing   **B** computing   **C** stock control

9 Michael thinks that more volunteers are needed in . . .
A charity shops.   **B** hospitals.   **C** schools.

10 Which job is NOT mentioned in the listening passage?
A librarian   **B** taxi driver   **C** lawyer

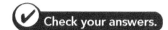 Check your answers.

2 🎧 **26** **Listen again and complete the table. Write no more than three words for each answer.**

Name of volunteer	Ayesha	Michael
Responsibilities	sorts books, serves customers, works on the **(1)** _____	provides **(4)** _____ for elderly people
Reasons for volunteering	enjoys **(2)** _____ in order to improve **(3)** _____	he missed **(5)** _____
Personal successes	appeared in a **(6)** _____, _____	recruited **(7)** _____ new volunteers, has made **(8)** _____ trips
Benefits	organised a **(9)** _____	sense of **(10)** _____
Suggestions for the future	encourage local councils to provide furniture, for example, **(11)** _____	provide more information about volunteering **(12)** _____

 Check your answers.

Pronunciation sentence stress

1  **27 Listen to the questions and underline the stressed words.**

1 Did you know that more than 22 million people in the UK currently volunteer?

2 Do you know that the value of their contribution is over 40 million pounds a year?

3 What do you actually do?

4 And what about you, Michael?

5 Have you had a particularly proud moment during your volunteering career?

6 What do you think are the main benefits of volunteering?

✔ Check your answers.

🎧 **27 Now listen again and practise, paying attention to the stressed words.**

Language study relative clauses

1 **Complete the passage. Use these words. Put in commas where necessary.**

that   where   which   who   whose

SPONSOR A CHILD. MAKE A DIFFERENCE.

There are 650 million children **(1)** _____ is more than ten times the UK population **(2)** _____ live on less than 60 pence a day. There are some developing countries **(3)** _____ poverty kills 1 in 3 children. They die from lack of food and diseases **(4)** _____ include dysentery and diarrhoea. Their lack of education means they have little opportunity to learn skills **(5)** _____ could help them find employment. Without help today, these children may never have the chance to improve their lives.

World Vision **(6)** _____ is one of the world's leading development charities, is helping to stop this through their child sponsorship programme. Your support will provide vital help to a child **(7)** _____ basic needs are clean water, basic health care and food. Your help will also provide education for a child **(8)** _____ will help to break the cycle of poverty.

It is children **(9)** _____ represent the future and child sponsorship is the best way to help communities. Make a difference and sponsor a child for as little as 60p a day **(10)** _____ is the cost of a soft drink.

2 **Complete the passage on page 69. Use these phrases.**

A who lives in Bangladesh

B who have vision so poor they cannot lead a normal life

C who was blinded by cataracts,

D who are blind

E which has flown to 80 countries

F which caused a terrible cyst to grow on her left eye.

G which can be treated with a donation of only £15.

H where they were able to watch Momena's operation.

I and to help train local doctors to save 665 more children in need

J that allowed him to see her for the first time ever

Many children in developing countries can't see because they are born with conditions like cataracts, **(1)** _____

We don't just cure cataracts. Momena Begum, **(2)** _____, has Goldenhar's syndrome, **(3)** _____ Our doctors were able to save her eye. Her eyes are clear now – to read, to study – it's wonderful.

We use donations to save the sight of girls like Momena. She wants to study and become an engineer. And her eye surgery will save others. We invited local doctors to our Flying Eye Hospital **(4)** _____ Our hospital, **(5)** _____, has run 220 sight-saving missions since 2002.

Dr Ali Al-Ani describes a moment when a 10-year-old boy, **(6)** _____ was able to see for the first time in his life. 'The young boy looked around and then looked at his mother. There was silence for a moment, then he said something to her. She burst into tears, and so did the boy. I ran to get a translator as I was worried. The translator slowly turned to me and said, 'Don't worry'. The child had told his mother that this was the first time he could see her. He said she was beautiful.

A donation of £15 provided eye surgery **(7)** _____. Sadly, there are still over 45 million people worldwide **(8)** _____ and another 135 million **(9)** _____. Your donation of £15 can change the world for a child with congenital cataracts. Your donation will be used for surgery **(10)** _____.

Please help us save a child's sight today.

Check your answers.

Writing | IELTS tasks: general training module task 1

1 **Read the question and underline the key words.**

> You should spend about 20 minutes on this task.
>
> *You are a college student. Your College Principal has asked you to help organise a student party at the college in aid of charity. Write a letter to the College Principal. In your letter . . .*
>
> *1   accept the invitation.*
> *2   suggest a suitable location for the party.*
> *3   offer to help with some aspect of the party.*
>
> *You should write at least 150 words. You do not need to write your own address. Begin your letter as follows:* Dear Mr Ogilvy,

 Check your answers.

Now read the letter below and put the paragraphs in order.

 Check your answers.

A I would be happy to organise the catering. I think I can encourage our canteen to donate some food so that we can make plenty of sandwiches and salads for the buffet. I will also make sure the students on the food technology course volunteer to help put some hot food on the menu too. _____

B I think it would be a good idea to hold the party in the sports hall as we can make use of all the space for eating, drinking and dancing. _____

C Yours sincerely, Paul Webb _____

D Thank you for your kind invitation to help organise a fundraising party at the college. I would be delighted to help raise money for Oxfam, which is a charity many students here already support. _____

E Thanks once again for your invitation to help and I look forward to hearing from you soon. _____

 Check your answers.

2 Read the following letter. There are 18 errors in the letter. Look at the underlined errors and correct them.

Dear Ms Lipp,

Thank you for your offer to <u>working</u> as a volunteer in our bookshop. I am very pleased that you are interested <u>to</u> helping to raise money for Oxfam, <u>that</u> is a charity many other students from your college already support.

There <u>is</u> many different ways in which you can <u>do</u> a contribution to the work of the shop, from helping customers to <u>sort</u> the books. There are also plenty of <u>opportunity</u> for you to be creative. One of our volunteers <u>enjoy</u> doing the window displays and I know that she would appreciate some additional help with this. You might also want <u>helping</u> organise special events in the shop. Recently we run a science fiction book week <u>where</u> was very successful. We are always happy to encourage our volunteers to take part in <u>organise</u> events like this.

Many of our student volunteers choose <u>work</u> at weekends <u>which</u> they have more free time. You can contribute as much or as little time to the shop as you want. However, could you tell me if you would like to <u>working</u> on weekdays or in weekends? The shop is open from 9am to 5pm every day <u>include</u> Sundays.

Thanks once again for your kind offer <u>helping</u> in our bookshop and I look forward to hearing from you soon.

<u>Your</u> sincerely,
Gareth Swann
Shop Manager

 Check your answers.

Now underline useful expressions in the letter.

3 Write a reply to the charity shop manager. Say which tasks you would like to do in the shop and when you would like to work.

1 We often use some verbs and nouns together – this is called *collocation*. Match the verbs with the nouns to make collocations.

verb	noun
meet	a difference
make	people
give	sure
learn	use
make	money
give	a charity
make	new skills
raise	a donation
make	time
support	two pounds

✓ Check your answers.

Now complete the sentences using a collocation.

1 Give water. Give life. **(1)** <u>*Give two pounds*</u> a month to Water Aid.

2 Do you have a few free hours every week? If you do, **(2)** _____ to Oxfam. Call into your local shop and have a chat with the manager.

3 Charity shop volunteers **(3)** _____ such as stock control and shop management. They also have the opportunity to **(4)** _____ and be part of a team.

4 If you want to change the world, don't just sit there – do something! Call today and find out about Oxfam's campaigns and the actions you can take to **(5)** _____.

5 A regular donation can help Water Aid change lives. **(6)** _____ online or call 020 7793 4594. **(7)** _____ you have your bank details ready.

6 Donate things you don't need to Barnardos. From computers to clothes to foreign currency, Barnardos can **(8)** _____ of your unwanted items.

7 Many people **(9)** _____ for charity by organising fundraising events in their local communities. These can range from sponsored parachute jumps to sponsored walks.

8 To me, being a volunteer means you really have to **(10)** _____ you are working for and believe in the cause. Then you know you are really making a difference.

Unit 11

Work

1 Match the jobs of the future 1–5 with job descriptions A–E.

A We need a caring and reliable person who can look after 1,500 elderly residents. ____

B We need someone with excellent communication skills to help parents choose the sex and personal characteristics of their new baby. Have you got what it takes to help parents-to-be? ____

C We need someone to check our global supply chains and to make sure we do not buy from companies who are polluting or are too carbon costly. ____

D We need a qualified mechanic experienced with a wide range of personal robots to carry out repairs and maintenance. ____

E We need someone to keep a group of people working from home happy, making sure that no one watches too much TV. ____

 Check your answers.

2 Read the passage about the jobs of the future. Match sections A–E with jobs 1–5 in activity 1.

A Given the choice, I'd never do it. I know that the technology is almost certain to become reality in the future but it's a very controversial area. I wouldn't feel comfortable if I had to help them choose things like intelligence or looks. ____

B I think this job would be fascinating. This area of business is one which is becoming increasingly important, as companies will be taxed more and more for polluting. I would also enjoy the opportunity to do something which helps the environment. ____

C Over the next twenty years many more people will be working from home instead of the office. But they are likely to feel a bit lonely. All I'd have to do would be to cheer them up and make sure they are working. If I did it for a long time though, it would get a bit boring. ____

D I'd be quite interested in this kind of job. This is a rapidly changing market with constant new development in this area of technology, from machines to do the vacuuming to one that chooses your clothes for the day. I don't know what the salary is – it doesn't say – but if it was well paid, I'd certainly do it. ____

E Oh, I think that there will always be a need for the human touch – despite more jobs being taken over by robots. After all, the face of a metal robot wouldn't have the same effect as the face of a caring nurse. If I could choose my hours and the salary wasn't too bad, I'd definitely consider it. ____

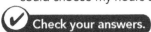 Check your answers.

Now underline examples of second conditional forms in A–E.

 Check your answers.

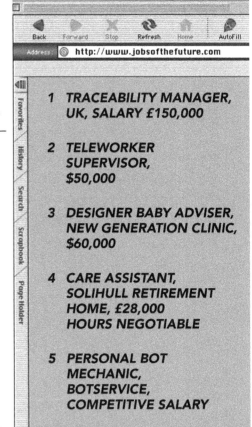

http://www.jobsofthefuture.com

1 TRACEABILITY MANAGER, UK, SALARY £150,000

2 TELEWORKER SUPERVISOR, $50,000

3 DESIGNER BABY ADVISER, NEW GENERATION CLINIC, $60,000

4 CARE ASSISTANT, SOLIHULL RETIREMENT HOME, £28,000 HOURS NEGOTIABLE

5 PERSONAL BOT MECHANIC, BOTSERVICE, COMPETITIVE SALARY

3 Complete the sentences with the verbs in brackets.

1 I _____ the job of a designer baby adviser even if it _____ well paid. (do/be)

2 I _____ being a care assistant if I _____ my hours of work. (consider/choose)

3 If the salary _____ good enough, I _____ into the area of mechanical technology. (be/go)

4 I _____ for a job in supply checking if it _____ helping the environment. (apply/involve)

5 I _____ working as a teleworker supervisor if it _____ boring. (continue/become)

✔ Check your answers.

Pronunciation second conditional

1 🎧 28 **Listen to the sentences and notice how the voice rises and falls.**

1 I wouldn't feel comfortable if I had to help them choose things like intelligence or looks.

2 If I could choose my hours, and the salary wasn't too bad, I'd definitely consider it.

3 If it was well paid, I'd certainly do it.

4 If I did it for a long time though, it would get a bit boring.

🎧 28 **Now listen again and practise.**

Vocabulary

1 **Complete the passage. Use the words below.**

skills   personal occupations   job seeker   job market   interview
employer   CV   advertisement   achievements

CV ADVICE

Your CV is an essential career document needed to present yourself effectively in the **(1)** _____. A good CV will considerably increase your chances of getting a face-to-face **(2)** _____ by highlighting relevant **(3)** _____, experience and value to a potential **(4)** _____.

There are no rights and wrongs when it comes to writing and presenting a **(5)** _____, and each document will be as individual as the **(6)** _____ it belongs to. However, by following some basic principles you will be able to present the information in a clear, concise and persuasive way.

You may need to put together more than one CV if you intend to apply for different **(7)** _____ across different sectors. This will enable you to emphasise the particular **(8)** _____, skills, experience and **(9)** _____ qualities that a particular employer is looking for. It is usually possible to tell what an employer is looking for from the job **(10)** _____ or job description: alternatively, you may need to research the role and the company yourself to ensure that your CV has the right focus.

 ✔ Check your answers.

1 🎧 **29 Listen to a careers officer. Write *true*, *false* or *not given* next to the statements below.**

1 There are generally two different types of CV. _____
2 Employers spend approximately five minutes reading a CV. _____
3 Previous jobs should always be described in detail. _____
4 A CV should consist of a maximum of two pages. _____
5 A typed CV creates a better impression than a hand-written one. _____
6 It is preferable to produce a CV on white paper. _____

2 🎧 **29 Listen again and complete the table and the notes. Write no more than three words for each answer.**

Type of format	Description of format	Advantage of format
Historical	lists employment details (1) _____	demonstrates (2) _____
(3) _____	emphasises individual talents and skills	details everything (4) _____

CV Checklist – things to remember

- Be (5) _____
- Focus on (6) _____ instead of (7) _____
- Include all other relevant skills such as (8) _____ and (9) _____
- Be accurate with (10) _____
- Obtain a (11) _____
- Choose (12) _____ stationery.

 Check your answers.

3 Choose the correct answer A–D.

1 Which are not discussed during the talk?
 A references
 B responsibilities
 C achievements
 D skills

2 Who would be most interested in listening to this talk?
 A a careers adviser
 B an employer
 C an undergraduate
 D a student counsellor

 Check your answers.

1 Read the passage and choose the most suitable headings for paragraphs A–H from the list of headings below. There are three extra headings.

List of headings

1	Be aware of your body language	**Paragraph** A	___
2	Questions to avoid	**Paragraph** B	___
3	Careful listening	**Paragraph** C	___
4	After the interview	**Paragraph** D	___
5	Anticipate questions in advance	**Paragraph** E	___
6	Review your application	**Paragraph** F	___
7	Plan what to wear	**Paragraph** G	___
8	Know where you are going	**Paragraph** H	___
9	Correcting yourself		
10	Don't talk too much!		
11	Be consistent		

✓ **Check your answers.**

Interview Essentials

The research you did for your application will help you get that job interview. Now do your homework on some interview essentials!

A Look back over your form and make a list of points that the interviewer is likely to want to talk about. Think particularly about how you will deal with any weaknesses or gaps in qualifications or experience. Make sure that you have solutions on offer, for example, showing that you have enrolled on a course that would give you what you are missing.

B Think about how long you need to get to the interview and what parking arrangements there are. If you park on the employer's premises, remember your car says a lot about you – so at least make sure it is clean. If you drive a noisy old vehicle, it may be better to make the journey by bus.

C Make a good impression. Do your best to look good. If you know you look good, you'll feel more confident. Smart and simple is best, whatever the job. You need to look as if you have made an effort for the interview. Clean shoes make a big difference.

D Most interview questions are predictable. Make a plan about what you are going to say, but don't memorise a script. Fix in your mind points you want to make, but what you actually say should be influenced by the type of people you are talking to and the clues you pick up from them.

E The most important interview skill is never to interrupt your interviewer. Make sure you understand every question you are asked; if you don't, ask for an explanation. If you are faced with something you really can't answer, then be

honest. Use phrases like 'that's something I'd need time to think about' or 'that's outside my present experience'.

F Many interviewers ask the same things in different ways as a means of checking information you have given. If you feel you made a mistake, put things right by saying *going back to what I said earlier . . ., what I really meant was . . . .*

G If there are awkward silences when you have finished, don't fill them with nervous talk. Some interviewers use silence to see how you'll react. Pass the lead back to them by pleasantly saying 'Does that answer your question?'

H Looking at your interviewer in the eye is essential, but don't do it too much. A smile sets everyone at ease, but a constant grin is unnerving. Sitting up straight and leaning forward to listen and talk all make you look attentive and enthusiastic.

2 Now read the passage again and circle the correct letter A–E.

1 The passage is from a . . .
  A brochure.
  B poster.
  C booklet.
  D prospectus.
  E journal.

2 Who would be most interested in reading this text?
  A a graduate
  B a school pupil
  C a psychologist
  D an employer
  E a careers advisor

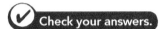 Check your answers.

Study skills collocation with *make* and *do*

1 Put the words and phrases in groups.

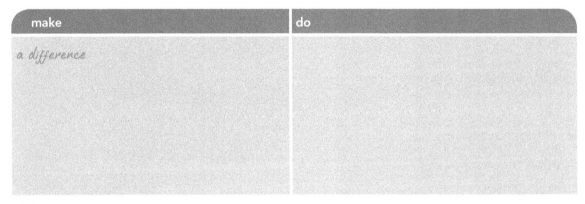

a difference   a list   a mistake   a plan   a point   an effort   an impression
homework   ironing   a journey   research   sure   your best

make	do
a difference	

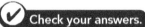 Check your answers.

1 Read the question and underline the key words.

> Many people are now asking whether it is necessary to transport people to work every morning and home every evening. Wouldn't it be cheaper to move the work to the people? Home working represents the future of work. How far do you agree with this view?

Now read the answer and correct the underlined mistakes.

Most developed <u>countrys</u> are now experiencing a transportation crisis. Roads and highways <u>is</u> packed with cars, parking spaces are rare and pollution <u>are</u> a serious problem. Strikes and breakdowns are common and transport costs are increasing all the time. These rising costs are met by individual workers. But of course they are passed on to the employer in the form <u>in</u> higher wage costs and to the consumer in higher prices.

In recent years there <u>have</u> been a vast increase in the number of people working from home. This means that employees work from home and keep in touch via laptops and mobile phones. Home working has many benefits for the employee. It <u>involve</u> less travelling to work, more leisure time, a better home and family life, reduction in stress and financial savings. Employers <u>to</u> save on office space, reductions in absenteeism, greater efficiency and better recruitment. <u>In</u> a result, they are moving out of offices in increasing numbers.

However, although home working may be cost effective and lead to greater efficiency, there are a number of problems <u>associate</u> with this kind of flexible working. Workers may, for example, feel isolated at home and miss the human contact of the office.

In balance I think that the key question is: when will the cost of installing and operating telecommunications equipment fall below the present cost of <u>commute?</u> While petrol and other transport costs <u>is</u> rising dramatically, the price of telecommunications is decreasing <u>considerable</u>. At some point <u>on</u> the near future, home working will be the norm.

Now write your own answer to the essay question. You have 40 minutes.

Unit 12

Academic success

Study skills   exam preparation

1 **Read the passage and match questions 1–5 with paragraphs A–E.**

1   I always panic as I sit down to do an exam. Can you help me get over this please?   _____

2   What's the best time of day to do revision?   _____

3   I'm finding it really hard to get motivated to do revision. Any advice?   _____

4   What type of food can I eat to help me concentrate?   _____

5   I have dreams that I'll forget to turn up for an exam. What would happen if I did?   _____

 **Check your answers.**

Exam Success

A   Different people have different concentration patterns. When do you feel most awake and aware? You should do most of your revision then. It's a bit inconvenient in the middle of the night but it works for some people. But be sure that you get enough sleep.

B   If you don't go, there's nothing that can be done. So make sure you have a good alarm clock by your side. Check that you have the right timetable and that you know what time each exam starts and allow plenty of time for buses and trains to be late. Actually, this is a very common dream to have, but it rarely happens.

C   If you feel stressed, the easiest thing to do is take lots of deep breaths in and out. That will automatically calm

you down. Focus when you turn over the exam paper. Do make sure you read the question properly. A lot of marks are lost because people misread the question.

D   When you are de-motivated, it's easy to find excuses that stop you working. Take it stage by stage. Do half an hour's work and then give yourself a reward – it could be a cup of tea or a healthy snack. Don't do too much at once.

E   Well, the theory is eat oily fish. But it doesn't work immediately. Avoid fatty foods, soft drinks and too many carbohydrates.

Vocabulary

1 **Match the words with the definitions.**

| class project   lecture   presentation   practical work   seminar   registration   rehearsal   tutorial |

A   This is a large class, usually lasting around one hour, where a tutor talks about a subject and the students take notes. There is little or no opportunity to ask questions. This usually guides you through the course material by explaining the main points of a topic. _____

B   This is a small discussion group. A number of students join their lecturer or tutor to discuss a particular topic and exchange ideas. It usually lasts one to two hours. Attendance is often obligatory. _____

C This usually takes place weekly and lasts about one hour. You meet with a lecturer or tutor, either on your own or with one to three other students to discuss your own work (for example, the essay you are writing) or to cover a topic in greater depth. _____

D On many courses you will have workshops, e.g. laboratories on science courses. On some courses (e.g. geography) you may go on field trips away from the institution. You may work individually but more usually you will be part of a group. These classes are usually designed to give you hands-on experience of the theories you learn in other classes and to develop practical skills. _____

E This is a study of a particular subject over a period of time and undertaken by a group of students. If the group includes students from different countries, you may find you have different views about how work will be shared and decisions made. This can be a good way of learning about working in a multi-cultural environment. _____

F At the beginning of a course of study, students are required to make sure that their personal details (name, address and date of birth) are recorded on the database of their university or college. _____

G You may be asked to prepare a paper in advance and then present it to other students for discussion. _____

H When you want to remember some information before giving a talk, you can go through a process of practising it in advance, repeating all the information. _____

✔ Check your answers.

Language study gerunds and infinitives

1 Read the notes and complete them with a gerund or infinitive using the verbs in brackets.

INDEPENDENT STUDY

On any course you will have to do some work on your own. This usually involves **(1)** _____ (research) a topic and producing written work, or **(2)** _____ (give) a presentation at a seminar. This is an important part of UK academic culture and aims **(3)** _____ (help) you develop skills such as problem solving. It also allows you **(4)** _____ (study) a topic in more detail and will help you learn **(5)** _____ (express) your own ideas and opinions. When you start **(6)** _____ (read) a book or article, you may want **(7)** _____ (scan) the contents page, chapter headings and introductory sentences. This will enable you **(8)** _____ (understand) the structure and ideas that will be discussed. You can then continue **(9)** _____ (read) in detail. Try **(10)** _____ (take) notes as you read, starting with the title, author and any other reference information (e.g. date, publisher). Try to avoid **(11)** _____ (copy) out a section of the text. Put it in quotation marks, so that you can reference it if you want, **(12)** _____ (use) it in your work.

✔ Check your answers.

2 Now put the verbs into groups.

aim allow avoid continue enable involve learn start want try

Verbs followed . . .

1 only by *to*: _____ *aim* _____

2 only by *-ing*: _____

3 by both *to* and *-ing*: _____

✔ Check your answers.

Pronunciation -ing

1 🎧 **30** Listen and write the words.

🎧 **30** Now listen again and practise paying attention to the -ing/ɪŋ/ ending.

Reading IELTS tasks: multiple-choice questions; true/false/not given

1 Read the passage quickly and choose the correct letter A–D.

1 The writer finds it difficult to remember . . .
A dates.　　**B** names.　　**C** faces.　　**D** less common words.

2 The writer makes reference to . . . types of memory.
A 2　　**B** 3　　**C** 4　　**D** 5

3 What technique for improving memory is NOT mentioned in the passage?
A written prompts　　**B** puzzles　　**C** repetition　　**D** word association

 Check your answers.

Memory Matters

Words fail me. I was trying to think of a word the other day but it just wouldn't come. Now, what was it? It wasn't something difficult. They hardly ever are. No, the ordinary words are the worst, and some are impossible to retrieve. Last year, I had to write *versatile* on my notice board, which is fine for literary use but no good if you are talking about food. Of course, there are alternative words here whose meaning might be used – *adaptable* or *flexible*.

But listening to experts on numerous radio programmes recently, I have learnt that there are two sorts of memory – the fact-and-figure kind and the dreamy kind. The first allows you (or doesn't) to remember the name of someone if you ever bump into them, while the other takes you back to what you were doing when you first met them.

The other thing is that your mind prepares the memory in the brain but then sends it somewhere else for safe keeping, so that years later (or in my case minutes), you forget what you're doing in the middle of going upstairs to get your house keys.

On the upside, some memories are the ones your body remembers, like riding a bike, or, as I discovered last week, how to play the piano after 30 years of not even having thought about it. OK, I'm not the best pianist in the world but it's pretty good for someone who often forgets names.

The Americans are busy setting up what they call mind gyms, where people go and do puzzles together in an attempt to build up their neural connections, the idea being that you can't do much about your brain cells dying but you can get the ones that are still alive to say hello to each other. Although I have always done hard crosswords with no obvious improvement to knowing where my keys are, I do like the sound of this and have already started brushing my teeth with the wrong hand and committing long shopping lists to memory based on associative thinking.

2 Read the passage again. Do the statements reflect the claims of the writer?

Write　TRUE if the statement reflects the claims of the writer.
　　　FALSE if the statement contradicts the claims of the writer.
　　　NOT GIVEN if it is impossible to say what the writer thinks about this.

1 Simple words are more difficult to recall than complex words.　　_____

2 There are too many programmes which focus on 'memory' at the moment.　　_____

3 Memory enhancement techniques being used in America sound uninteresting.　　_____

 Check your answers.

3 Now choose the correct letter A–D.

1 The purpose of the text is to . . . the reader.
   A inform
   B entertain
   C warn
   D advise

2 The text is taken from a . . .
   A review.
   B journal.
   C text book.
   D newspaper article.

✓ **Check your answers.**

Listening IELTS tasks: multiple-choice questions; note completion

1 🎧 31 Listen to a talk and choose the correct letter A–C.

1 The main theme of the talk is . . .
   A teaching methods.
   B research methods.
   C study skills.

2 Lectures are designed to . . .
   A introduce new topics.
   B explore topics in depth.
   C clarify information contained in course books.

✓ **Check your answers.**

🎧 31 **Now listen again and complete the notes. Write no more than three words for each answer.**

- Don't write down everything.
- Focus on (1) _____
- Avoid writing down information such as (2) _____ or jokes.
- Use abbreviations and (3) _____
  they will help you (4) _____
- Keep your notes (5) _____

✓ **Check your answers.**

2 Do the statements agree with the information given in the listening passage?

Write   TRUE if the statement is true according to the passage.
        FALSE if the statement is false according to the passage.
        NOT GIVEN if the statement is not given in the passage.

1 The college used to operate an open-book exam system.   _____
2 Exams are held once a term.   _____
3 Few students made recordings of college lectures last year.   _____
4 Students must ask permission before recording lectures.   _____

✓ **Check your answers.**

1 Read the question and underline the key words.

> You are a student in a college and have not yet completed an important assignment for your course.
>
> You are writing a letter to your tutor. You should apologise for the delay, explain why the assignment is late and request an extension.

2 Write down three reasons students give for not completing work on time.

Now read the following letter and check if your reasons were included.

Dear Ms Cheng,

I am writing to apologise for not <u>complete</u> my project on Information and Communication Technology. I am extremely sorry for not <u>meet</u> the deadline you set and realise that the delay will cause you a lot of inconvenience.

<u>Although</u>, unfortunately, I have had domestic problems to deal <u>in</u> recently. My mother is currently recovering at home after <u>an</u> major operation and I need to look at her.

<u>On</u> view of this, I would be very grateful if you could allow me <u>having</u> more time to complete this important assignment. Ideally, I require an additional week so that I can proofread it and check my references. I also need <u>writing</u> up my conclusion but as I have already managed to prepare the outline of the summary, it should not <u>to</u> take too long.

Once again, I regret this extremely unfortunate delay but hope to submit it <u>in</u> the end of next week.

Yours sincerely,

Sara Melvin

3 Correct the underlined errors.

 Check your answers.

4 Read the letter again and underline any useful phrases.

5 Now write a letter to your teacher explaining why you missed a deadline for an assignment.

Answer key

Unit 1

Reading

1 1 E   2 B   3 A   5 F   6 G   C 7   8 D
2 A   C   F   G
3 1 D   2 B   3 A   4 C

Vocabulary

1 A bar graph   B pie chart   C flow chart
   D line graph   E table

2 1 C   2 E/columns/rows   3 D/vertical axis/horizontal axis
   4 B/segment   5 A/columns

3

noun	verb	adjective
admission	admit	admitted
administration	administer	administered
enrolment	enrol	enrolled
registration	register	registered

4 1 business   4 art and design   7 engineering
   2 agriculture   5 computing   8 languages
   3 architecture   6 biology   9 medicine

Listening

1 1 The student is talking on a mobile phone.
   2 He is standing outside the Finance Office.
   3 They pay their fees.
2 1 A   2 C   3 A   4 D
3 1 10.00   2 317   3 Bank   4 Lecture   5 Sports

Pronunciation

1 1 8   3 8   5 8   7 8   9 6
   2 8   4 7   6 8   8 9   10 5
2 1 Professor Cholmondeley
   2 Academic writing: http://www.uefap.co.uk
   3 Address: 13 Weatherspoon Avenue Bicester OX6 7LY
   4 Tutor's email: pat.smith@warwick.ac.uk
   5 Accommodation in De Rothschild Building

Language study

1 Suggested answers

   1 Anthony
   2 Frederick
   3 Jones
   4 My date of birth is 31st August 1993.
   5 I'm Australian.
   6 Do you mean my parents' address?
   7 They live at 15 Prospect Road, Adelaide.
   8 I'm staying in room 38, in the Harvey Building.
   9 I'm taking Business Studies.
   10 My personal tutor is Dr Frances Robinson.
   11 I'm a new student.
   12 Thank you. Where is the Finance Office?

2 1 Are/waiting   8 is registering
   2 are doing   9 are you doing
   3 'm/am waiting   10 don't/do not know
   4 do you come   11 Do you want
   5 come   12 are you going
   6 are you enrolling   13 are playing
   7 'm/am studying   14 'm/am meeting

Writing

1 1 bar   6 bicycle   10 segment/section
   2 transport   7 motorbike   11 Unibus
   3 Business   8 pie   12 yellow line
   4 bus   9 bus   13 5
   5 of

Unit 2

Reading

1 1 kindergarten   6 gap year
   2 elementary school   7 university
   3 junior high school   8 BSc
   4 high school   9 master's degree
   5 high school diploma

2 1 true   3 true   5 true   7 false
   2 not given   4 false   6 true   8 not given

Listening

1 1 government funded   4 kindergarten   7 fees
   2 private   5 public school
   3 boarding school   6 single sex

2 A   C   D

3   1 90 minutes   3 12   5 statue
        2 2.30   4 Illona Jarvis

Pronunciation

1   <u>stu</u>dents – 2   re<u>fec</u>tory – 4   en<u>joy</u>ing – 3
        <u>sun</u>bathing –3   <u>sil</u>ly – 2   <u>laugh</u>ing – 2
        to<u>wards</u> – 2   <u>opp</u>osite – 3   uni<u>ver</u>sity – 5

2   Oo – union, several, civic, bursar, private, lecture
        oOo – religious, admissions
        Ooo – atmosphere, government, workstation
        oOoo – postgraduate
        Oo is the most common stress pattern in these words

Language study

1   towards/up/into/into/along/to/out of/towards/across/to/
        through/past/to/over/in front of/across/between/towards/
        up/to

   Now complete the sentences.

        1 into   3 up   5 past   7 in front of
        2 across   4 into   6 towards   8 across

2   **Suggested answer:** . . . goes past the admissions office,
        up the stairs and into the library. Then he goes out of the
        library, down the stairs, across the square and stops in
        front of the refectory.

Vocabulary

1   1 Bursar's Office   6 lecture hall
        2 auditorium   7 student IT centre
        3 art gallery   8 nightclub
        4 International Office   9 cinema
        5 Student Information Centre 10 radio station

2

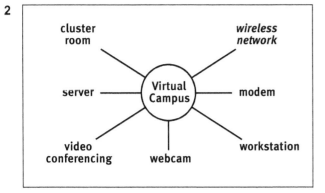

Writing

1   1 a sharp rise   3 a levelling off   5 a dramatic fall
        2 a slight increase   4 a gradual fall

2   You have <u>just started a course at university</u>. You <u>have
        left your MP3 player in a hotel</u> you stayed in for two days
        when you first arrived.

        Write a letter to the hotel manager. In your letter . . .

        • <u>explain</u> your situation
        • say <u>where</u> you left the MP3 player
        • tell the manager <u>what you would like him/her to do</u>

You should write at least <u>150 words</u>. You do NOT need to
write your own address.

Begin your letter *Dear Sir/Madam*.

The best order is:

A 1   D 2   F 3   B 4   E 5   H 6   G 7   I 8   C 9

3   Yours faithfully, Raymond Chan

4   1 B   2 C   3 A   4 D

Unit 3

Vocabulary

1   1 types of accommodation: bedsit, flat, hall of residence,
           shared house, apartment
        2 areas in accommodation: corridor, kitchen, foyer, toilet,
           porter's lodge
        3 people/jobs: caretaker, warden, landlord/landlady,
           porter, security staff, cleaner, flatmate, room mate

2   1 do: washing-up, washing, vacuuming, ironing
        2 make: bed, dinner, repairs

Reading

1   1 dep   3 pcm   5 all mod cons
        2 pw   4 ref   6 bed

2   1 D (it has parking)
        2 A (it has a wifi connection)
        3 C (it is fully furnished)
        4 B (for a non-smoking person)
        5 E (two bedrooms)

3   1 Because they are lost or locked in rooms.
        2 On campus.
        3 Because they are worried about their sons or daughters.
        4 Wardens, porters and security staff.

        1 mattress   3 opt
        2 parking permit   4 run smoothly

Language study

1   1 will start   4 will only have   7 will go   10 will have
        2 will pick up   5 will take   8 will get   11 will not be
        3 will probably   6 will see   9 will be
           forget

Now read the conversation again and complete the times.

        1 6.00   2 6.30   3 6.45   4 7.15   5 7.30

2   1 are you doing/am not doing/am having
        2 am coming/will give/will be
        3 Is Turgut arriving/is going

3   1 are going to be/will go
        2 it's going to rain/will just take
        3 will have

4 are we going to do/will talk
5 are we going to get/will look

Pronunciation

2 1 yes   2 no   3 no   4 yes   5 no   6 no

3 1 You must not/mustn't smoke.
2 You must not/mustn't play loud music.
3 You must hand in your essay by 6th December.
4 You must not/mustn't park here.
5 You must not/mustn't bring food and drink into the lecture.

Study skills

1 key word
2 stressed syllable
3 pronunciation
4 word type
5 definition
6 example
7 words that go together
8 revised/remembered columns

Writing

1 A   C   E

Now underline the phrases for making requests.

I . . . would like to get some further information from you. Could you send me a map of the city and the University?

Could you also arrange a parking space . . .?

I would also like to know . . .

2 You are going to start a course at a college in Australia. Write a letter to the admissions tutor. In the letter . . . say when and where you are arriving.

explain that you are not familiar with the city.

say what you need from the college.

Suggested answer
Dear Sir / Madam,

I am starting my course at your college on 23rd September and I would like to get some further information from you.

I will arrive on 20th September and would be grateful if you could send me a map of the city and college.

I would also like to know when I will be able to move into my room and where to collect the keys from.

I look forward to hearing from you.

Listening

1 1 C   2 D   3 A   4 B   5 E

2 1 B   2 A   3 C   4 B   5 C   6 B

Now complete the summary. Use these words.

1 chores
2 categories
3 entertainment
4 housework
5 team
6 ageing
7 human

Unit 4

Listening

1 1 He was expelled from Eton.   3 He met Lulu.
2 He had a telephone call.   4 He broke his neck.

2 1993 – D   1995 – G   1996 – J   2001 – A
2002 – I   2006 – F   2008 – C   2009 – E   2010 – H

Language study

1 1 She divorced Harry . . .
while she was living in Africa.
before she moved to Paris.

2 She married Jean-Paul . . .
after she divorced Harry.
while she was living in Paris.
before she studied art.

3 She won the lottery . . .
after she married Jean-Paul.
while she was studying art.
before she had an art exhibition.

4 She had an art exhibition . . .
after she won the lottery.
while she was working and bringing up the family.
before she learned to sing.

5 She learned to sing . . .
after she had an art exhibition.
while she was living in New York.
before Jean-Paul left her.

6 Jean-Paul left her . . .
after she learned to sing.
while she was singing in nightclubs.

2 Dona: We need some ideas about a film for tonight. Tao, what are your thoughts on this? Do you have any suggestions?
Tao: How about showing a Kung Fu movie?
Istvan: I'd like to suggest a romantic film. It's nearly Valentine's Day.
Dona: Good idea. Have you got any more suggestions?
Sara: We could show a horror movie.
Dona: I'd like to avoid doing that. Some of them are very violent.

1 have any suggestions
2 How about
3 any more suggestions
4 could
5 like to suggest
6 What are your thoughts

Reading

1 1 true   2 true   3 false   4 false   5 not given

2 C   F   E   A   G   B   D

3 1 The Accidental Spy
2 Another 24 hours To Die
3 Beyond Borders
4 About Schmidt
5 Along Came Polly
6 Boa
7 Solaris

Vocabulary

1
1 treasurer   4 secretary   7 funds
2 committee   5 vote
3 minutes   6 apology

Pronunciation

1
A 10 words   C 7 words   E 11 words
B 8 words   D 16 words   F 11 words

2
A <u>Three</u> hundred and eighty-<u>four</u> thousand, <u>eight</u> hundred and <u>two</u>
B <u>One million</u>, sixty-<u>eight</u> thousand and sixty-<u>nine</u>
C <u>fifty-seven</u> thousand, <u>five</u> hundred and <u>thirty</u>
D <u>One billion</u>, <u>seven hundred million</u>, <u>eight</u> hundred and thirty-<u>six</u> thousand, <u>seven</u> hundred and forty-<u>two</u>
E nine million, <u>four</u> hundred and <u>fifty</u> thousand, <u>four</u> hundred and thir<u>teen</u>
F <u>seven</u> hundred and sixty-<u>two</u> thousand, <u>nine</u> hundred and eighty-<u>four</u>

Writing

1
1 2009 and 2010   3 *Avatar*
2 Three – Action, Comedy and Drama

2 D   F   C   E   A   G   B

Suggested answer

In this category, the amount of profit in 2010 was less than in 2009. The *King's Speech* made only £237,676,627, while *Inglourious Basterds* made £320,351,773 the year before.

Study skills

1
1 stu.dent   3 *n = noun*   5 etc.
2 /stjuːdənt/   4 *esp*

2
1 studious   3 study (v)   5 studied
2 study (n)   4 studio

Unit 5

Reading

1
1 reporter   3 key   5 applicants
2 freelance   4 occasional   6 links

2
1 false   3 false   5 true
2 true   4 not given

Vocabulary

1
1 press   6 stock
2 radio   7 electronic
3 broadcasting   8 foreign
4 news   9 government
5 communication   10 computer

Pronunciation

MSc – Master of Science
IELTS – International English Language Testing System
ISBN – International Standard Book Number
BA – Bachelor of Arts
CD ROM – Compact Disc Read-Only Memory

Study skills

1
1 photographer/photo(graph)   3 photography
2 photographic

2
1 With a ' before the syllable
2 'photograph   pho'tographer
photo'graphic   pho'tography

Language study

1
1 Harold Jakes has never worked as a sports journalist.
2 Has Harold Jakes ever lived in America?
3 Harold Jakes has reported for the BBC since 1992.
4 Candace Weingold has always worked in America.
5 She has done some live reporting.
6 She has never worked on a music programme.
7 Has Candace done a degree in media journalism?
8 Both Harold Jakes and Candace have worked in media for more than ten years.
9 Neither of them have ever had experience as an anchorman.

2 Suggested answers
1 Doctors have finally found a cure for the common cold.
2 The Americans have landed on Mars.
3 A woman from Manchester has had five baby boys.
4 Manchester United has won the cup!

3
1 This is because of global warming.
This is the effect of global warming.
This is caused by global warming.

2 This is because of the earlier introduction of satellite TV.
This is caused by the earlier introduction of satellite TV.
This is the effect of the earlier introduction of satellite TV.

3 This is because of cheaper production.
This is caused by cheaper production.
This is the effect of cheaper production.

4 This is because of the popularity of broadband.
This is caused by the popularity of broadband.
This is the effect of the popularity of broadband.

5 This is because they watch too much television.
This is caused by too much television.
This is the effect of too much television.

Reading and listening

1 1 true   2 not given   3 true   4 true

2
1 too old   5 American
2 DJs   6 sports
3 live reporting   7 newspaper
4 a degree   8 media studies

Writing

Dear Sir or Madam,

I have seen your advertisement on the Internet for a receptionist, and I am interested in applying for the job. I am 22 years old and live in South London. I have recently completed a course in Media Studies at Maidstone College, and achieved a good pass on the course. My tutors say that I have a good personality, and I make friends easily. I am hoping to become a production assistant in the future, and the careers counsellor at the college has advised me to take an office job first, because this way I can learn how a production company is organised.

I hope you will consider my application. I have enclosed my CV, and you can see that I have some experience of office work and good computer skills. I am available for interview at any time.

I look forward to hearing from you.

Yours sincerely,

Sweehar Wing

Unit 6

Reading

1 1 W 2 C 3 C 4 W 5 W 6 C 7 W
    8 W 9 C 10 W

Vocabulary

1 1 hand in   3 show   5 do
    2 deadline   4 handout   6 break

2 1 D 2 B 3 E 4 C 5 A

3 1 Office: administrator, receptionist
    2 Academic: professor, research assistant

Listening

1 1 D/E 2 A 3 D/E 4 C 5 B
    A D F

2 1 charity organisation 4 bedrooms   7 Eco-friendly
    2 on the roofs   5 back garden
    3 60%   6 shop

Language study

1 2 Computers are shared by all the residents.
    3 Enough heat and light (light and heat) is generated for
      82 houses.
    4 Some of the houses are reserved for local workers.
    5 A similar project is already planned.
    6 Bicycles are used by most of the residents.

2 1 A 2 P 3 P / A 4 A 5 P

Reading

1 1 fission   2 fusion
2 A 4   B 6   C 2   D 1   E 7   F 3
3 1 true   2 true   3 false   4 not given   5 false
4 1 radioactive fallout   3 laser
    2 by-product   4 fossil fuel

Study skills

1 1 fission/fusion   4 turbine/generate   7 dam/pump
    2 electric power   5 current
    3 geothermal   6 fuel/pollute

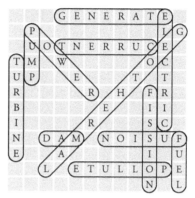

Pronunciation

1 workstation, turbine, geothermal
2 report, transformer
3 current, pump, hub, combustion
4 pollute, do, fuel, nuclear

Writing

1 Second, the intake, where gates on the dam are opened and water is pulled through the penstock – a pipe that leads to the turbine. Water pressure is built up as it flows through this pipe. Third, and perhaps the most important component, is the turbine. The turbine houses large blades, which are hit by the water and are attached to a generator above it through a drive shaft. The most common type of turbine for hydropower plants is the Francis Turbine, which looks like a big disc with curved blades.

2 1 In order to   4 At the next stage   7 by
    2 Firstly   5 so that
    3 so as to   6 Finally

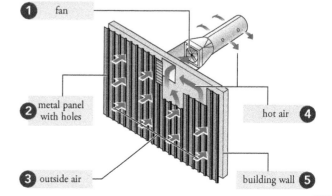

Unit 7

Vocabulary

1
1 pleasant   4 terrible   7 modern
2 humid   5 overcrowded   8 dynamic
3 dirty   6 coastal

Language study

1
1 easier   4 faster
2 better   5 more pleasant
3 more expensive

Now complete the passage using the correct superlative form of the adjectives in brackets.

1 cheapest   3 best   5 most beautiful
2 most pleasant   4 fastest

Reading 1

1 1 C

Now complete the table.

1 transport costs   3 resources
2 energy consumption   4 farmland

2
1 society   5 a small part
2 More than half   6 growth
3 over ten million   7 increases
4 economically   8 differences

Listening

1 1 C   2 B   3 A   4 C

2
1 well-lit   5 close to you
2 waste ground   6 route
3 facing the traffic   7 hear (the) traffic
4 dropped/it is dropped   8 behind (you)

3 1 B   2 A   3 B

Pronunciation

1 1 9   2 10   3 9   4 10   5 9   6 9
7 12   8 9

2
1 much better to be   6 far more important than
2 in some larger   7 you can be seen more
3 no more than   easily
4 will be less than   8 much safer to
5 it's better to

Writing

1
1 The chart shows how people like spending their free time in the city according to age.
2 77 (young), 11 (older)
3 68 (young), 3 (older)

2 comparing: 5 6   contrasting: 2 4   classifying: 1 3

Study skills

1

Classifying	Contrasting	Comparing
to make a distinction between … and… to divide the information into…	however… in contrast with	to have in common similarly in comparison with… compared with as…as in the same way likewise

Unit 8

Vocabulary

1 1 C   2 A   3 E   4 F   5 G   6 B   7 D

2
1 call   5 information   9 charged
2 screen   6 premium rate   10 prizes
3 keypad   7 cost
4 key   8 key word

Reading

1
1 false   3 not given   5 false
2 true   4 false   6 true

2
1 stretching   4 leftover response
2 oxygen   5 contagious
3 social

Listening

1 1 C   2 B   3 C   4 C   5 B   6 A
7 B   8 A

Now listen again and complete the notes using no more than three words.

1 unique
2 postcode
3 NT42 9WA 7
4 out of sight
5 turn it off OR turn off OR switch it off OR switch off
6 report it/report it immediately/tell the police.

2 1 mark   2 use   3 lose

Language study

1 If you take a few practical steps, you can't go wrong.
If your phone goes missing, report it to the police.
If you go to a DIY shop, you can buy a marking kit.
If you don't need to use your phone, switch it off.

2
1 in case   4 in case of   7 Unless
2 If   5 If   8 if
3 if   6 if   9 in case

Pronunciation

1 If you take a few practical steps, you can't go wrong.

2 If your phone goes missing, the police can identify it.

3 If you press – star – hash – zero – six - hash, you can find out your phone's unique number.

4 Try to keep your phone out of sight if you are walking on the street.

Writing

1 What are the <u>advantages</u> and <u>disadvantages</u> of having a <u>mobile phone</u>?

You should write at least <u>250 words</u>.

2 1 D   2 F   3 G   4 C   5 B   6 H   7 I
    8 A   9 E

Study skills

1 1 reference books   5 magazines
   2 lending service   6 Internet
   3 professional journals   7 DVD player
   4 newspapers   8 digital resources

Unit 9

Vocabulary and reading

1 1 sailing   3 fencing   5 football   7 lacrosse
   2 cricket   4 rowing   6 handball   8 basketball

2 1 improve your flexibility   3 body building
   2 jogging, walking and rowing

Study skills

1 A	2 K	3 G	4 H	5 B	6 I
7 F	8 D	9 L	10 J	11 C	12 E

Reading

1 1 C   2 B   3 C

2 A 5   B 2   C 1   D 3   E 4

3 1 true
   2 false
   3 true
   4 false
   5 false (in fact, the opposite)

Now read the passage again …

1 Measuring how much oxygen a person is taking into the body; measuring the heart rate.

2 Start with a walk of just five minutes.

3 Any physical activity, no matter how small.

Language study

1 1 should   2 shouldn't   3 should   4 should   5 shouldn't

2 1 must be a member   2 must have a training session
   3 must not smoke   4 must not use MP3 players

3 **Suggested answers**

1 He shouldn't watch so much TV. He should take up a sport.

2 He shouldn't drive to work. He should walk to work.

3 He shouldn't eat fast food. He should eat healthy food.

4 1 will   2 might/may   3 can/might/may (also could)
   4 can/will   5 will

5 100% certain to be, 75% likely to be, 60% probably, 50% possibly

Now complete the passage.

1 are likely   3 possibly
2 are certain to be   4 probably

6 1 could hurt yourself   2 can suffer from dehydration
   3 can/could hurt your knees and feet   4 could make things worse

Listening

1 A 3   B 5   C 1   D 2   E 4

2 1 C   2 B   3 A

3 1 B   2 B   3 C

Now answer the questions.

1 in place of war and to settle arguments and for religious reasons.

2 There were no rules or protective clothing.

3 Canada.

Writing

In the last century, many people did things by hand, but nowadays more and more tasks have become automated. For example, many people have washing machines, clothes driers and dishwashers, so the amount of energy needed to wash and dry clothes and wash dishes is greatly reduced. As technology progresses, more and more of these tasks will be automatic, for example, vacuum cleaning or cutting the grass. In addition to this, improvements in technology have given us 24-hour a day entertainment from digital TV to video games. This means that there are fewer tasks to do, more time to do nothing and more opportunities to sit around and be entertained without moving very much.

As we can see, there are both advantages and disadvantages to this. I will deal with the advantages firstly. I think there are at least two positive effects of this. First of all, we do not need to do repetitive and uninteresting jobs like washing-up and this gives us more time to do other things. What we do with this time depends upon the individual. Secondly, for people who are less able to do these jobs, like elderly or disabled people, these machines are a great help. Future developments may be able to help them even more. I think that this is the most positive side of technology.

Now I will look at the disadvantages. As I mentioned, it is up to the individual what they do with this extra time. Unfortunately, instead of doing everyday tasks, people tend to watch television or play video games. Furthermore, television companies encourage us to watch as much TV as possible. This can lead to an inactive lifestyle and people becoming overweight and unhealthy.

In conclusion, the positive side is that because machines and automation do the things we do not like doing, we gain more time to do other things, and people who cannot do certain things are able to do them with the help of technology. However, on the negative side we lose the daily activity involved in washing-up, vacuum cleaning and so on, and for some people, this may be the only kind of activity they do. The danger is that we do not replace these activities with others.

Unit 10

Vocabulary

1 1 D   2 B   3 A   4 C

2
1 contribute	4 volunteer	7 campaign
2 fund	5 support	8 charity
3 donation	6 poverty	

Now complete the passage.

1 development	4 donation	7 support
2 poverty	5 contribute	8 charity
3 funds	6 volunteers	

Reading

1 1 C   2 D   3 A   4 B   5 E

Now write …

1 (chance to) travel, meet (new) people, gain (new) skills, flexible

2 do research/research on the Internet, build a website

3 National Volunteering Centre, websites, Do-it website

2
1 gain new skills	5 full-time
2 travel	6 Voluntary Service Overseas
3 new skills	7 Do-it
4 time	

Listening

1 1 C   2 C   3 B   4 A   5 A   6 B   7 B
    8 C   9 B   10 C

2
1 till	7 25/twenty-five
2 books	8 1,000
3 (her) CV	9 Welsh writers' week
4 transport/lifts	10 community
5 contact with (new) people	11 bookcases and photocopiers
6 newspaper	12 opportunities

Pronunciation

1 Did you <u>know</u> that more than <u>22 million people</u> in the UK currently <u>volunteer</u>?

2 Do you <u>know</u> that the <u>value</u> of their <u>contribution</u> is over <u>40 million pounds</u> a year?

3 <u>What</u> do you <u>actually do</u>?

4 And <u>what</u> about <u>you</u>, Michael?

5 Have you <u>had</u> a particularly <u>proud</u> moment during your <u>volunteering career</u>?

6 What do you <u>think</u> are the <u>main benefits</u> of <u>volunteering</u>?

Language study

1
1 , which	5 which/that	9 who
2 , who	6 , which	10 , which
3 where	7 whose	
4 which/that	8 which/that	

2 1 G   2 A   3 F   4 H   5 E
    6 C   7 J   8 B   9 D   10 I

Writing

1 You should spend about <u>20 minutes</u> on this task.

You are a college student. Your <u>College Principal</u> has asked you to help <u>organise a student party</u> at the college in <u>aid of charity</u>.

<u>Write a letter</u> to the College Principal. In your letter …

1 <u>accept the invitation</u>.
2 <u>suggest a suitable location</u> for the party.
3 <u>offer to help with some aspect of the party</u>.

You should write at <u>least 150 words</u>. You do not need to write your own address. Begin your letter as follows:

Dear Mr Ogilvy,

Now read the letter and put the paragraphs in order.

D   B   A   E   C

2 Thank you for your offer to <u>work</u> as a volunteer in our book shop. I am very pleased that you are interested <u>in</u> helping to raise money for Oxfam, <u>which</u> is a charity many other students from your college already support.

There <u>are</u> many different ways in which you can <u>make</u> a contribution to the work of the shop, from helping customers to <u>sorting</u> the books. There are also plenty of <u>opportunities</u> for you to be creative. One of our volunteers enjoys doing the window displays and I know that she would appreciate some additional help with this. You might also want to help organise special events in the shop. Recently we ran a science fiction book week which was very successful. We are always happy to encourage our volunteers to take part in organising events like this.

Many of our student volunteers choose to work at weekends when they have more free time. You can contribute as much or as little time to the shop as you want. However, could you tell me if you would like to work on weekdays or at weekends? The shop is open from 9am to 5pm every day including Sundays.

Thanks once again for your kind offer to help in our bookshop and I look forward to hearing from you soon.

Yours sincerely,

Study skills

1 make a difference, make a donation, make use, give time, raise money, learn new skills, meet people, give two pounds, make sure, support a charity

   Now complete the sentences using a collocation.

   1 Give two pounds   6 Make a donation
   2 give time   7 Make sure
   3 learn new skills   8 make use
   4 meet people   9 raise money
   5 make a difference   10 support a charity

Unit 11

Language study

1 1 C   2 E   3 B   4 A   5 D
2 A 3   B 1   C 2   D 5   E 4

   Now underline examples of second conditional forms in the comments above.

A I'd never do it/I wouldn't feel comfortable if I had to help them choose things like intelligence or looks.

B I think this job would be fascinating/I would also enjoy the opportunity to do something which helps the environment.

C All I'd have to do would be to cheer them up and keep an eye on them and make sure they are working!/If I did it for a long time though, it would get a bit boring.

D I'd be quite interested in this kind of job/if it was well paid, I'd certainly do it.

E the face of a metal robot wouldn't have the same effect as the face of a caring nurse. If I could choose my hours and the salary wasn't too bad, I'd definitely consider it.

3 1 wouldn't do … was
   2 would consider being … could choose
   3 was …, 'd go

   4 'd apply for … involved
   5 wouldn't continue … became

Vocabulary

1 1 job market   5 CV   9 personal
   2 interview   6 job seeker   10 advertisement
   3 skills   7 occupations
   4 employer   8 achievements

Listening

1 1 true   3 not given   5 not given
   2 false   4 true   6 true

2 1 in chronological order
   2 career progression
   3 skills-based
   4 you can do
   5 confident/positive
   6 achievement/achievements
   7 responsibility/responsibilities
   8 IT or language *or* (a) driving licence
   9 IT or language *or* (a) driving licence
   10 spelling and grammar
   11 second opinion
   12 good quality

3 1 A   2 C

Reading

1 A 6   B 8   C 7   D 5   E 3   F 9
   G 10   H 1

2 1 C   2 A

Study skills

1

make	do
a difference	homework
a list	ironing
a mistake	research
a plan	your best
a point	
an effort	
an impression	
a journey	
sure	

Writing

1 Many people are now asking whether it is necessary to transport people to work every morning and home every evening. Wouldn't it be cheaper to move the work to the people? Home working represents the future of work. How far do you agree with this view?

2 Most developed countries are now experiencing a transportation crisis. Roads and highways are packed with cars, parking spaces are rare and pollution is a serious problem. Strikes and breakdowns are common and transport costs are increasing all the time. These rising costs are met by individual workers. But of course they are passed on to the employer in the form <u>of</u> higher wage costs and to the consumer in higher prices.

In recent years there <u>has</u> been a vast increase in the number of people working from home. This means that employees work from home and keep in touch via laptops and mobile phones. Home working has many benefits for the employee. It <u>involves</u> less travelling to work, more leisure time, a better home and family life, reduction in stress and financial savings. Employers <u>save</u> on office space, reductions in absenteeism, greater efficiency and better recruitment. <u>As</u> a result, they are moving out of offices in increasing numbers.

However, although home working may be cost effective and lead to greater efficiency, there are a number of problems <u>associated</u> with this kind of flexible working. Workers may, for example, feel isolated at home and miss the human contact of the office.

<u>On</u> balance I think that the key question is: when will the cost of installing and operating telecommunications equipment fall below the present cost of <u>commuting</u>? While petrol and other transport costs <u>are</u> rising dramatically, the price of telecommunications is decreasing <u>considerably</u>. At some point <u>in</u> the near future, home working will be the norm.

Unit 12

Study skills

1 1 C   2 A   3 D   4 E   5 B

Vocabulary

1 A lecture   E class project
    B seminar   F registration
    C tutorial   G presentation
    D practical work   H rehearsal

Language study

1 1 researching   7 to scan
    2 giving   8 to understand
    3 to help   9 to read
    4 to study   10 taking/to take
    5 to express   11 copying
    6 reading/to read   12 to use

2 1 verbs followed only by *to*:
       aim allow learn want enable

    2 verbs followed only by *-ing*:
       involve avoid

    3 verbs followed by both *-to* and *ing*:
       continue start try

Reading

1 1 B   2 A   3 C
2 1 true   2 not given   3 false
3 1 B   2 D

Listening

1 1 A   2 A

    Now listen again.

    1 main points/important details
    2 examples or stories/examples/stories
    3 symbols
    4 write faster/write more quickly
    5 in order/in a file

2 1 not given   2 not given   3 false   4 false

Writing

1 You are a student in a college and <u>have not yet completed an important assignment</u> for your course.

    You are writing <u>a letter to your tutor</u>. You should <u>apologise</u> for the delay, <u>explain</u> why the assignment is late and <u>request an extension</u>.

3 Dear Ms Cheng,

    I am writing to apologise for not <u>completing</u> my project on Information and Communication Technology.
I am extremely sorry for not <u>meeting</u> the deadline you set and realise that the delay will cause you a lot of inconvenience.

    <u>However</u>, unfortunately, I have had domestic problems to deal with recently. My mother is currently recovering at home after a major operation and I need to look <u>after</u> her.

    <u>In</u> view of this, I would be very grateful if you could allow me <u>to have</u> more time to complete this important assignment. Ideally, I require an additional week so that I can proofread it and check my references. I also need <u>to write</u> up my conclusion but as I have already managed to prepare the outline of the summary, it should not to take too long.

    Once again, I regret this extremely unfortunate delay but hope to submit it <u>at/by</u> the end of next week.

    Yours sincerely,

    Sara Melvin

4 I am writing to apologise for/I am extremely sorry/… realise that the delay will cause you a lot of inconvenience/ In view of this, I would be very grateful if you could allow me to have more time/Once again, I regret this extremely unfortunate delay but hope to submit it in the end of next week.

Audioscripts

Unit 1: On course

Listening

🎧 1

Simon: Hi Hiroko, it's Simon. I'm on my new mobile phone.

Hiroko: Hey, that's great. Where are you, Simon?

Simon: I'm outside the Finance Office. I've just paid my fees. Where are you?

Hiroko: I'm in my room, still waiting for my parents to phone, but I think it's too late now. I think it's nearly time for them to go to bed in Japan. My father gets up very early in the morning, because he has to travel to Tokyo on the train every day. What are you doing?

Simon: I'm coming to see you! I want to talk about the timetable for Tuesday. I know what we are doing, but I don't know where all the different places are yet.

Hiroko: I haven't got a timetable. Where can I get one from?

Simon: They have them in Admissions. We can go there later and get another copy for you.

Hiroko: I really need to go shopping. Is there any time for me to go to the supermarket?

Simon: Not until Wednesday afternoon. Wednesday afternoon is always free for sports. Wednesday morning we have a talk from the head of the Students' Union, about the sports programme.

Hiroko: OK, that should be interesting. What time is the first lecture tomorrow?

Simon: The first lecture is at two o'clock in the afternoon, it's about the Bank of England. But there's a welcome meeting before that, at ten.

Hiroko: Where is the meeting?

Simon: It's in the Business School, room 317.

Hiroko: All right. Let me write that down. Business School, room 317. Do you know where that is? I know where the Business School is, but I don't know where room 317 is.

Simon: Not really. I want to go there now and find it. And the lecture is in the Grantham lecture theatre. Do you know where that is?

Hiroko: Er . . . no. No idea.

Simon: Right. Well I'm going to the Business School to look for both these places. Are you coming with me?

Hiroko: OK. I'm putting my jacket on. Oh, where are my keys? All right, I've got them.

Simon: You don't need a jacket. It's quite warm today. Walk towards the Finance Office – I'm standing outside the [mumbles]

Hiroko: What's that? I can't hear you.

Simon: Sorry. I'm eating a bag of crisps. There's a snack machine here and I'm really hungry. Registration is very tiring. I'm outside the main door of the Finance Office. Are you still there? What time does the canteen open?

Hiroko: I think it's open now.

Simon: Let's have lunch first then. I'm starving. Hurry up!

Pronunciation

🎧 2

1 I'm not seeing her at all today.

2 He's waiting for you in the registry.

3 Do you want to join the chess club?

4 They're taking the bus to Leicester.

5 I'm not taking the test this morning.

6 Does she really want to study at Nottingham?

7 Is he still going out with that girl?

8 There isn't any reason why you can't.

9 What time does the canteen open?

10 Who are you waiting for?

3

1   That's right, your tutor's name is Professor
    Cholmondeley. C H O L M O N D E L E Y.

2   You can find information on academic writing on the
    internet, at the following website: H T T P colon backslash
    backslash W W W dot U E F A P dot co dot U K

3   And where do you live?

    My address is number 13, Weatherspoon Avenue, that's
    W E A T H E R S P O O N Avenue, Bicester.

    How do you spell Bicester?

    B I C E S T E R

    and the postcode?

    It's O X 6 7 L Y

4   You may contact your tutor by email. The address will be
    first name dot last name at Warwick dot A C dot U K, so
    Dr Smith will be P A T dot S M I T H at W A R W I C K dot
    A C dot U K.

5   Your accommodation will be in the De Rothschild
    building.

    I'm sorry, could you spell that for me?

    Yes, of course. It's spelt D E, then another word,
    R O T H S C H I L D. De Rothschild.

 4

1   Cholmondeley. C H O L M O N D E L E Y.

2   H T T P colon backslash backslash W W W dot
    U E F A P dot co dot U K

3   13, Weatherspoon Avenue

    W E A T H E R S P O O N Avenue, Bicester.

    B I C E S T E R

    O X 6 7 L Y

4   P A T dot S M I T H at W A R W I C K dot A C dot U K

5   De Rothschild.

    D E, then another word, R O T H S C H I L D.

Unit 2: Campus

Listening 1

 5

Although there is a government-funded free education
system in Canada, some people prefer to choose private

education for their children, believing that smaller class
sizes and a different approach will give their children a
better start in life. There are currently more than 1700
private or public schools in Canada with around 8% of
students attending them. Many wealthy and prominent
people choose not to send their children to state schools,
but send them to private schools instead. Some schools
are single-sex – that is for either boys or girls only, but
many are changing to being co-educational, that is for both
sexes.

There are some private religious schools in Canada, and
these are mainly Hindu, Sikh, Muslim, Jewish and Christian.
Many state schools are Catholic, so there is not a big
demand for private Catholic schools.

Many families choose to send their children to a boarding
school. This is a place where pupils live at the school,
receiving all their meals and sleeping there. Boarding schools
may take children from kindergarten at age five through to
18 when they can take the International Baccalaureate, or
the high school diploma. Many private high schools require
students to take an entrance examination and attend an
interview with their parents before they are given a place at
the school.

The elite private schools are called public schools and
are usually attended by children of the very wealthy.
One of the most famous public schools in Canada is
Upper Canada College in Toronto. Many of the students
come from overseas. Sons and daughters often attend
the same schools their mothers or fathers went to. The
fees at these schools can only be afforded by the very
wealthy.

Listening 2

 6

Administrator:	Hello, how can we help you?
Illona:	I'd like to go on the tour of the campus and I was hoping I could get some details from you.
Administrator:	Sure. How long are you here for?
Illona:	Well, I'm leaving this afternoon but hopefully I'll be back in September.
Administrator:	Right, now you've missed the 10.30 tour with Chris, but if you hurry you'll just be able to catch the 12.30 tour.
Illona:	I think that's a bit early – I was hoping to get a bite to eat in the refectory before I went on the tour.
Administrator:	Good choice – there's a Mexican theme today – I hope you like Mexican food. So the

next one is at 2.30 and the final one sets off at 4.30.

Illona:	How long does the tour last?
Administrator:	About 90 minutes.
Illona:	In that case I think the 4.30 tour might be too late for me – I need to catch a train around half past five.
Administrator:	So the 2.30 tour then.
Illona:	Great.
Administrator:	Let me check – we have a maximum number of 12 people so that everyone can have a chance to ask questions or get information they need. And there are still four places left, so I'll put you down for that one.
Illona:	That's great.
Administrator:	So what's your name?
Illona:	Illona – that's I-double L-O-N-A, Jarvis – J-A-R-V-I-S.
Administrator:	Now I'll need to give you a visitor's pass and this tour ticket to give to the guide when you meet him – his name's Dean.
Illona:	OK.
Administrator:	Where did you hear about the tour?
Illona:	I saw it in the information pack.
Administrator:	Oh, good.
Illona:	And where does the tour start from?
Administrator:	Go out of the main entrance of the Richmond building and wait at the statue.
Illona:	Thank you very much.
Administrator:	Enjoy the tour, and see you in September.

Pronunciation

 7

between   students   refectory   enjoying   sunbathing
silly   laughing   towards   opposite   university

 8

union   religious   atmosphere   several   civic
admissions   bursar   private   government
postgraduate   workstation   lecture

Pronunciation

 9

I think I'll go on my bike.

We'll just take our waterproof coats.

I'll talk to him.

I'll look at the map.

Listening

 10

Presenter:	In today's talk, we're going to hear about something a lot closer to home – the future of housework. So, without any further delay, I'd like to invite Professor Reinhardt to give today's talk.
Professor Reinhardt:	Hello, and good afternoon. Today's talk is about the future of the way we live, but it's also about how we live today, because in many ways the future of housework is already with us. Before I go on to explain what I mean, let me bring in the main theme of this lecture – the role of technology in the home. We all dislike doing certain day-to-day tasks like vacuuming and cutting the grass, so what if we could give these jobs to someone who doesn't mind doing them? I don't mean a cleaner, either. I'm talking about a robot. By robot I mean a machine with sensors and microprocessors equipped with simple artificial intelligence which can do repeated tasks without the need for human help. Now, you will already have realised that this definition includes many household machines and devices that we already use – for example, your DVD player, or your microwave. In fact we can divide the robots we use and will use more frequently in the future into five categories: entertainment robots, appliance robots, immobots, assistive robots and androids. Let's have a look at entertainment robots first. Today, many toys include microprocessors and sensors. A good example is Dasarobot's pet robot dog, Genibo, which uses sensors to identify its surroundings, can take photos and can express emotions and interact with its owner. Appliance robots have more useful functions; iRobot's Roomba is a vacuum cleaner that automatically cleans your room. It has a sensor that stops it hitting furniture and an infrared eye that stops it falling down the stairs. There are now over 20 manufacturers of robotic

vacuum cleaners. Imagine a home where you don't need to vacuum any more because your robot helper does it. There is also an Automower by Husqvana that cuts the grass. In contrast to these moving robots are immobots: robots that rarely move, but work in teams in fixed positions around the house. For example, when your alarm rings, immobots will tell the coffee maker to get your coffee ready, ask the outside immobot to check the weather, then the outside immobot will tell your wardrobe immobot to choose light clothes for you in hot weather, or rain clothes in wet weather. Another example of this is the intelligent fridge – a refrigerator that tells you what you need and in the future will place your shopping order with the supermarket. The global market for the software for these immobots is estimated at $99 billion today, but will reach around $138 billion in the near future. The next category is assistive robots – robots which help people. These are already here with cars that have seats that slide out to help the driver get in, or robot arms that can carry and lift things for us. Companies are developing exoskeletons: suits made of steel and plastic that people can wear to increase their physical strength. With an ageing population, the market for assistive robots is very large, and researchers think that 40% of adults will wear some kind of computer within the next ten years. Our final category is the most difficult kind of robot to produce – a human robot that moves and acts like us – an android. Japanese companies are at the forefront of android research and Professor Ishiguro of Osaka University has developed a life-like robot called the Actroid that can smile, blink and move like a human. However, the reality of a robot that can behave exactly like a human is not here quite yet. Nevertheless, a company in England predicts that by 2020 there will be 55.5 million robots in the world – many of them domestic robots in a market worth $59 billion.

Unit 4: Film society

Listening

 11

Bob: And now, the moment you've all been waiting for, my very special guest Mr Harry Harpoon, movie star!

Harry: Hi, pleased to be here.

Bob: Harry, I believe you started out in life with a very good education.

Harry: That's right, Bob. I was an Eton boy until the age of 16. Then I'm afraid I got into a bit of trouble, and it was – let's see – 1992 when I was expelled.

Bob: Expelled? What for?

Harry: Just general bad behaviour, I suppose. But everything changed when I met Cindy, in the following year. It was love at first sight. She was an artist – still is – and a very successful one, too.

Bob: But you didn't marry Cindy until two years later, did you?

Harry: Right again, Bob. We got married in 1995, two years after I'd met her.

Bob: Why the delay?

Harry: I think it was because neither of us really believed in marriage at that time. Of course all that changed when the baby came along.

Bob: And it was one year later when you made your first movie, *Captain Sam*. Tell us about that.

Harry: OK. I was working as a model for an agency in London, when I was spotted by Dicky DuBarry, and he offered me the part. I told him I had no acting experience, but he said that didn't matter, the face was right and I could learn the rest as we went along. And that's what I did. Making *Captain Sam* was a great experience, but after that I had no more acting work for several years, and I thought my career was over. I had always wanted to travel, so in 2001, Cindy and I went to Africa with Robby, who was six. We tried to settle down there, but Cindy found the life too tough, and one year later, we divorced.

Bob: How long did you stay in Africa?

Harry: Another four years. Then the phone rang, and it was Dicky again. 'Harry,' he said, 'I've got a part that's just made for you!'

Bob: And that was the leading role in *Hello, Saturday*.

Harry: Yup, that's the one. I made enough money to move to Barbados, and a year after I'd moved there I met Lulu. I met her and married her in the same year – 2009. Now there are two women in my life – Lulu and my beautiful daughter, Mandy.

Bob: But then there was a setback.

Harry: There certainly was. The following year, I was horse riding in Colorado, when a bear suddenly appeared in front of us. The horse reared up, I fell off, and next thing I knew I was in hospital with a broken neck. But it's all right now, the doctors say I can work again soon, and Dicky's already got a new movie he's very excited about.

Bob: Well, we'll all look forward to that. Harry, thanks for coming in today.

Harry: My pleasure, Bob.

Pronunciation

 12

A   three hundred and eighty-four thousand, eight hundred and two

B   one million, sixty-eight thousand and sixty-nine

C   fifty-seven thousand, five hundred and thirty

D   one billion, seven hundred million, eight hundred and thirty-six thousand, seven hundred and forty-two

E   nine million, four hundred and fifty thousand, four hundred and thirteen

F   seven hundred and sixty-two thousand, nine hundred and eighty-four

 13

As track 12.

Unit 5: Bulletin

Pronunciation

 14

MSc

IELTS

ISBN

BA

CD-ROM

 15

Producer: OK, so these are the two most promising CVs we've got so far. Let's start with Harold Jakes. Hmm ... What do you think?

Director: Well, the first thing I noticed was his date of birth. Perhaps he's a little bit too old to take on such a demanding job. I mean – 1955!

Producer: Careful, Jan. We don't want to be accused of ageism. Older people have more experience.

Director: Yes, he's got plenty of that, but it isn't the kind of experience we need, is it? His only experience as a radio producer was for a local music programme. We're not looking for a DJ, we already have plenty of those.

Producer: It says here that it was also a local news and phone-in show. He's done a lot of time as a journalist.

Director: That's true, but most of it has been behind a desk. We need somebody who can report the news as it happens – breaking news. Has he done anything like that?

Producer: Well, it says here that he was a presenter for the BBC. That probably involved some live reporting – but we can't be sure. But you haven't mentioned what I see as the most serious problem – he's British. How would the listeners react to that? We're an American Public Radio station, our audience isn't used to foreign presenters.

Director: Well, we do speak the same language, after all. But I know what you mean ... it could be a problem. I don't know. I think his voice sounds great on the tape he sent us.

Producer: The other thing that worries me is his lack of qualifications. He doesn't have a degree.

Director: They probably didn't have degrees in journalism when he was starting out in his career. You had to learn through experience – and I think that's probably the best way.

Director: Let's have a look at the other one – Candace Weingold. Now she's an all-American girl. And she's younger than Mr Jakes, isn't she?

Director: Yes, she is. Much younger. The main problem with Candace seems to be that most of her experience is connected with sports journalism. That really isn't what we're looking for.

Producer: I agree, but she has done some live reporting and she's had a job as producer, for WDET.

Director: Yes, but since 2005 she's worked for a newspaper. Most of her career has been writing, not speaking on the radio. I wonder why? Have you listened to the CD she sent with her application?

Producer: Not yet – I've got it here somewhere. She has good qualifications, though. A BA in Media Studies from a good university. She's also worked for a Public Radio Station, like ours, in Detroit.

Director: Yes, that's definitely an advantage. Shall we listen to that CD? Have you found it yet?

Producer: Yup, here it is. I'll put it on ...

Candace (recorded):   ... and now for the latest news from the Masters golf tournament. It's Tiger Woods again ...

Producer: Oh my! Maybe some voice training could help?

Unit 6: Energy

Listening

 16

Interviewer:	... and now for something entirely different. I've got Felicity Campbell here in the studio today. She's one of the first people to move into BedZED, an eco-friendly housing development in south London. Welcome to the programme, Felicity.
Felicity:	Thank you.
Interviewer:	So, please tell us something about the place where you live. When did you move into BedZED, and how do you like living there?
Felicity:	I moved in in April 2002, just after the building was finished. I love living there. I had always wanted to have a more 'green' lifestyle. Now I can live without feeling guilty about polluting the environment.
Interviewer:	Can you tell us something about the history of BedZED?
Felicity:	Oh, yes. BedZED was designed by the architect Bill Dunster, for a joint venture between the Peabody Trust and BioRegional, which is an environmental charity organisation. Their goal was to create a self-contained living centre which used no energy and produced no carbon emissions. All the energy used in BedZED is generated by solar panels on the roofs of the buildings.
Interviewer:	Great!
Felicity:	Yes. Sunlight is turned into electricity by these solar panels. It's wonderful – there are few electricity bills to pay, as the houses are so well insulated that they only use 40% of the power that conventional houses use.
Interviewer:	So, even in the British climate it's possible to generate enough solar power to provide light and heat for ... how many houses are there?
Felicity:	Enough light and heat is generated for 82 homes. They range from one-bedroom flats to four-bedroom houses. Mine is a three-bedroom house
Interviewer:	What kind of people live there?
Felicity:	All kinds. Because the development was built by a charity organisation, some of the houses are reserved for local key workers, such as teachers and nurses. Some are leased at a low price to people on social security. Others who live there are young professionals who work from home. Instead of back gardens, BedZED has shared workstations where computers are shared by all the residents. The gardens are on the roofs!
Interviewer:	I'd love to see this place.
Felicity:	Well, you can. There are tours every Wednesday and Friday, but don't bring your car. There's nowhere to park.
Interviewer:	Where do you park your car?
Felicity:	I haven't got one. Most of the residents use bicycles, or public transport. Cars do so much damage to the environment – I feel great about not having one. And besides, we have a shop, a nursery and a café inside the development. You never need to leave!
Interviewer:	Do you think that the success of BedZED will mean that more projects of this kind will be built in future?
Felicity:	A similar project is already planned. There is a waiting list for houses – everybody wants to live there. Perhaps property developers will realise that there is a huge market for eco-friendly accommodation, and start to build this kind of property.
Interviewer:	Well, thank you for talking to us, Felicity. How are you getting home?
Felicity:	On the train! It's been a pleasure.

Pronunciation

 17

Sound 1: [ɜː] Example: her, workstation, turbine, geothermal

Sound 2: [ɔː] Example: more, report, transformer

Sound 3: [ʌ] Example: but, current, pump, hub, combustion

Sound 4: [uː] Example: food, pollute, do, fuel, nuclear

Unit 7: Cities

Listening

 18

Good afternoon, everyone. My name's Tim Risebrow and welcome to the second session of our college orientation programme. Now, let's move on from personal safety on

campus, which we covered in the first session, to keeping safe when we're out and about. Now, we take your safety both inside and outside the college very seriously indeed and feel that it is vital that you know how to protect yourselves. So, how can we stay safe in the city?

Now, many of our students walk back home to campus in the dark, particularly at weekends when there is lots going on in the city centre. And while we want you to make the most of the night life in Birmingham, you need to take a few simple precautions to protect yourselves. Firstly, remember to stay away from dark, lonely streets and stick to well-lit areas as much as possible. Try not to take short cuts through, for example, parks and waste ground, even if it means adding a few extra minutes to your journey home. After all, it's much better to be safe than sorry. It's also important to walk facing the traffic if you can. This means a car cannot pull up behind you unnoticed.

Now, many of our students carry personal attack alarms when they go out at night. There are a few on sale in our college shop and you can also find them in some larger DIY stores in the city centre. They cost no more than a couple of pounds. However, make sure that you buy one that will continue sounding even if it is dropped or falls on the ground. Also remember to keep it where you can get to it easily – don't leave it at the bottom of your bag! In an emergency, it will be less than useful there! All in all, it's better to carry it in your hand so that you can use it immediately.

On the subject of bags, carry them close to you with the clasp facing inwards. Avoid putting your house keys in your bag, carry them in your pocket instead. However, if the worst happens and someone tries to grab your bag, let it go immediately. Always remember that your own safety is far more important than your property.

Now, many of our students go jogging and cycling. It's a good idea to vary the routes you take as often as you can. In parks, always keep to the main paths and open spaces where you can see and be seen more easily by other people. So it's better to avoid wooded areas too. One final point – be careful when you use your MP3 player when you are out and about. When you are wearing one, you can't hear traffic or someone coming up behind you. So, it's much safer to leave it at home. Now, any questions before we move on to keeping safe on buses and other public transport?

Pronunciation

 19

1 It's much better to be safe than sorry.

2 You can also find them in some larger DIY stores.

3 They cost no more than a couple of pounds.

4 In an emergency, it will be less than useful there.

5 It's better to carry it in your hand.

6 Your safety is far more important than your property.

7 Keep to the main paths where you can be seen more easily.

8 It's much safer to leave it at home.

 20

1 much better to be

2 in some larger

3 no more than

4 will be less than

5 it's better to

6 far more important than

7 you can be seen more easily

8 much safer to

Unit 8: Communication

Listening

 21

Presenter: Just about everyone seems to have one these days. Yes, you've guessed it – I'm talking about a mobile phone, of course. But it seems that owning one carries a high degree of risk – if you read the latest crime statistics at least. We're running a risk simply by carrying our mobile phones on the streets. Did you know that a mobile phone is stolen in half of all street robberies? And in two thirds of these robberies, a mobile will be the only item taken? Now that's the bad news but the good news is the police are fighting back with a mobile phone crime prevention campaign. And Crime Prevention officer Roz Thorpe is here to tell us all about it! Hello there Roz.

Roz: Hello. Indeed, we think everyone should be aware of the mobile phone crime prevention campaign. If you take a few practical steps, you can't go wrong. So here is some simple advice that we can all follow to keep our mobiles safe. First of all, you should make sure you record your IMEI number.

Presenter: IMEI number?

Roz: Yes, your IMEI number. Now this is the number which is unique to every mobile phone. So write down your IMEI number in case your phone is stolen. So if your phone goes missing, the police can identify it. This means that they can prove it belongs to you!

Presenter: Good advice there, Roz. So how can we find out our IMEI number, exactly?

Roz: Well, it's easy. If you press star-hash-zero-six-hash, you can find out your phone's unique number.

Presenter: Hash-star …

Roz: No, STAR, hash, zero, six, hash.

Presenter: Star, hash, zero, six, hash.

Roz: Then, of course, you mustn't forget to have your phone property marked. Property marking provides you with even more protection in case of theft or loss.

Presenter: Property marking? What's that?

Roz: Well, this means marking your phone with your postcode and the number of your house or flat. If you look online, you can pick up a marking kit for a couple of pounds. You can also get a special etching or engraving tool. So, if your phone is stolen the police can identify it more easily. Now you should mark your phone using the postcode, followed by your house number. As you can see, I've marked mine, like this NT42 9WA 7.

Presenter: Some useful advice, there, Roz. Anything else mobile users out there have to remember?

Roz: Yes! Many of us have our mobiles on show when we are out and about and we really don't have to. Try to keep your phone out of sight if you are walking on the street. And obvious though it sounds, unless you actually have to use your phone, keep it turned off. You shouldn't keep it on unnecessarily. And one final point, make sure you report it missing immediately if it is lost or stolen.

Presenter: Some good tips there. Now, Roz, as part of your mobile phone crime prevention campaign, you've come up with great eye-catching posters to remind us all to be more aware of the risks, haven't you?

Roz: Yes, if you lock it, mark it, keep it, use it – you won't lose it!

Presenter: Right now, Roz, in case some listeners have just tuned in … what's the advice again?

Roz: One more time, just for you. Lock it, mark it, keep it and use it.

Presenter: Thank you very much, Roz.

 22

If you take a few practical steps, you can't go wrong.

If your phone goes missing, the police can identify it.

If you press – star – hash – zero – six – hash, you can find out your phone's unique number.

Try to keep your phone out of sight if you are walking on the street.

Unit 9: Fitness and health

Pronunciation

 23

You should put your clothes in a locker.

You should ask a member of staff.

You shouldn't begin exercising immediately.

Students must be a member.

Students must have a training session.

Members mustn't smoke.

Members mustn't use MP3 players.

Listening

 24

OK, now let's do our final yoga position – it's the triangle, and it's called the triangle because the position we end up in is similar to a triangle. Let me explain how to do it before we start so that everyone has an idea of what is going to happen. So, we are going to start with our feet together and pointing forward. The next thing is to spread your feet about a metre apart and then turn your left foot 90 degrees to the left, so it's pointing out to the side. Now turn your right foot 45 degrees inward, so that it is pointing slightly away from your body. Breathe in and raise both arms out to the side, parallel to the floor. Breathe out slowly, turn your head round to the left and look down your arm so that you can see your fingers. Now stop and check your left knee is in line with your left foot. This is really important as you could hurt yourself if your knee and foot are out of line. Next, take a big deep breath, and stretch outwards to the left, bending your left hip down and your right hip up. Now, when you've stretched as far as you can, raise your arms – don't try to reach your ankle yet, let your left hand rest against your calf, while your right hand points straight up. Turn your head and look up at your right hand. Now breathe deeply in and out for several breaths. Stay relaxed. Stand up straight, put your hands on your hips and pivot your heels, moving your feet back to the front. Finally, breathe out again and bring your feet back together. And that's it – the triangle. Everybody clear? OK, let's try it.

 25

Hello everyone, and thanks for coming to the second talk at the University of Victoria's School of Physical Education. Today I'm going to look at Canada's national sport, sometimes known as the fastest game on two feet – lacrosse. In contrast with many sports, no one really knows when, or how lacrosse started. This is because the sport was originally played by American Indians or Canadian First Nations people centuries ago.

When European settlers first came across the game, it had few, if any, rules. Lacrosse games could last for days, stopping when the sun went down and starting again the next day. There was no limit to the number of people in a team, often there were as many as one thousand players in a lacrosse game at the same time. Because there were no rules and players did not wear any protective clothing, many players suffered frequent and severe injuries.

This brings me to my first point – the use of lacrosse in place of war. The game was particularly violent when it was used in place of war to settle an argument or dispute.

The second purpose of lacrosse was religious. For many of the early players, a lacrosse competition was a replay of the story of the creation of the world and of the struggle between good and evil. Europeans first saw the game in the 17th century. One theory of how the game got its name is that the French saw the Huron people playing the game and called it *la crosse* as the stick used to throw the ball looked like a cross carried by French bishops. A century later, Europeans started playing the game, and it became an Olympic sport in 1904 in the Olympics at St Louis.

Unit 10: Charities

Listening

 26

Presenter: Did you know that more than 22 million people in the UK currently volunteer? And do you know that the value of their contribution is over 40 million pounds a year? Sounds impressive enough doesn't it? But the government is aiming to improve on those figures. They want to encourage more of the young and not so young to sign up for involvement in good causes. In fact, they want to attract more new recruits from the over-fifty age group over the next year. Two volunteers from both ends of the age spectrum are with us this evening – Michael Stubbs and Ayesha Choudhray. A very warm welcome to you both.

Michael: Thanks.

Ayesha: Thank you.

Presenter: Now, Ayesha, if I can start with you. Talk us through your work as a volunteer. What do you actually do?

Ayesha: Well, I work in a charity bookshop here in North Wales. I basically do anything and everything from sorting the science-fiction books to working on the till! I've been working there since it opened three years ago, in fact. I originally saw an appeal for volunteers in an empty shop window, volunteered myself and the manager, Gareth, asked me to come and help him set up the shop. There was already another branch of Oxfam but it had over seventy volunteers, so being involved in getting the first Oxfam bookshop off the ground here seemed very exciting. I've always been keen on books – my mum's a librarian too – and so I thought I'd grab the chance! And, of course, like most other students, I thought it would look good on my CV!

Presenter: And what about you, Michael?

Michael: Well, I run a community transport scheme which provides transport for elderly and disabled people who need lifts to and from local hospitals and health centres. I'm a retired policeman and when I stopped working four years ago I realised just how much I missed being in contact with other people. So, I decided to help out with the scheme and before long I found myself running a group of volunteers myself!

Presenter: Ayesha, have you had a particularly proud moment during your volunteering career?

Ayesha: Well, I suppose it would have to be the day the shop opened for the first time. I was really pleased to be involved in the build-up to the opening. I was even more proud when the opening was featured in our local newspaper and there was even a picture of me and our very first customer on the front page! And more recently I was lucky enough to come across a rare first edition – which later sold for £60!

Presenter: And what about you, Michael?

Michael: Well, I've managed to recruit twenty-five new volunteers to the scheme from all walks of life – doctors, taxi drivers, business people and even another policeman, like me! And last week, I made my 1,000th trip so that certainly gave us all something to celebrate!

Presenter:	What do you think are the main benefits of volunteering?
Ayesha:	Well for me one of the best things is working with other volunteers who turn up week after week in all weathers to raise funds for Oxfam. They're a great bunch of people. There's also plenty of scope to be creative. For instance at the moment I am organising a Welsh writers' week. And of course it gives you an opportunity to learn new skills like book-keeping and stock control.
Michael:	Well, for me the main benefit is the real sense of community among the volunteers and the people we help. It's also nice to know how much we are appreciated by their friends and relatives too.
Presenter:	What should be done to encourage more people to volunteer?
Ayesha:	Well I think the Government should put more pressure on local councils to help charities and voluntary organisations like ours by providing us with resources like old bookshelves or photocopiers.
Michael:	Ayesha's right, of course. I think also that people need to be more aware of the range of volunteering opportunities available to them. People generally think of Oxfam shops like Ayesha's, but there are hundreds of other things that you can get involved in – like helping disabled children to swim or visiting elderly patients in hospital. I think more work needs to be done to actually promote the options open to people.
Presenter:	Thanks for that, and after the break we'll be talking to …

Pronunciation

 27

1 Did you know that more than 22 million people in the UK currently volunteer?

2 Do you know that the value of their contribution is over 40 million pounds a year?

3 What do you actually do?

4 And what about you, Michael?

5 Have you had a particularly proud moment during your volunteering career?

6 What do you think are the main benefits of volunteering?

Unit 11: Work

Pronunciation

 28

1 I wouldn't feel comfortable if I had to help them choose things like intelligence or looks.

2 If I could choose my hours, and the salary wasn't too bad, I'd definitely consider it.

3 If it was well paid, I'd certainly do it.

4 If I did it for a long time though, it would get a bit boring.

Listening

 29

OK, come on in everyone. Let's get going shall we, because we've got a lot of ground to cover in today's session on CVs. So, let's make a start. As you all know, CV stands for Curriculum Vitae, and it is an essential document we all need to present ourselves effectively in today's job market. Now, there are no rights and wrongs when it comes to writing and presenting a CV, but by following a few basic golden rules you will be able to create the right impression to potential employers.

OK, let's think about presentation. Now, as you can probably guess, most employers see hundreds of CVs and yours may get less than a minute of their time. As we all know, first impressions count. Yes, first impressions are lasting impressions!

There are two main kinds of format that we can use to present ourselves on paper. Most people follow a historical CV format. This involves putting your employment history in chronological order. The main advantage of this is that it gives a good idea of career progression. However, some people opt for a skills-based CV format that highlights your abilities and skills. This can be useful as it gives you the chance to show what you can do rather than simply listing a series of jobs. So, whichever format you choose, your CV should look neat and tidy with all the information easy to find. But as you can imagine, there are lots of other dos and don'ts we should bear in mind before we even think about putting pen to paper!

First of all, it is important to sound as confident as possible and use positive language. Remember also to concentrate on your achievements rather than on your responsibilities. It's also important to make reference to other skills that could raise you above the competition such as a driving licence, IT skills or languages. And try to keep your CV to a maximum of two pages. And of course, it goes without saying that you should check your work for correct spelling and grammar. Spotting errors is a quick and easy way for employers to eliminate weaker candidates … especially when they have a mountain of CVs to read! It might be a good idea at this stage to encourage someone you trust to read over your CV too, so that you get a second opinion! Finally, although it is tempting to make your CV stand out by using bright coloured paper, it's best to stick to good quality white paper!

OK. Let's move on to content and see what you actually need to include on your CV.

Unit 12: Academic success

Pronunciation

 30

researching   giving   expressing   reading   taking copying

Listening

 31

OK, well let's make a start, shall we? Good morning, everyone. My name's Yusuf Khan and I'm the student counsellor. In this first session, I'll be giving you an introduction to the different teaching methods used here in the college and then after lunch we'll move on to study skills – so that you'll have some ideas on how to approach your own studies and research. As you'll be expected to do a lot of work on your own, it's useful to know how to manage your time and work effectively.

We use a number of different teaching methods here in the college – lectures being one of the most important, and you'll be timetabled for them from the very start of your courses here. As I'm sure you know, they are large classes – around one hundred students in some sessions!

Now, lectures are intended to guide you through the course material and present new topics which will be covered in greater detail during seminars, which we'll go on to later. And of course lectures will also provide you with the most up-to-date information that you may not get in the textbooks on your reading lists.

Now, when you attend lectures you'll need to take notes. But do remember that you don't need to write down everything the lecturer says. Try to concentrate on the main points and important details. The majority of the lecturers use asides or stories to illustrate a point, examples and even jokes. You don't, of course need to write all of this extra information down. It's a good idea to use abbreviations and symbols for more common words and terms when making notes. They can enable you to write faster but remember to use ones that you will understand later! If there is anything you don't understand, make a note to ask after the lecture.

Some of our lecturers invite questions from the floor during their sessions, so take the opportunity if you feel unclear about a point. It goes without saying that it is important to keep your notes in order in a file. Many of our students write up their notes neatly after lectures. This provides an opportunity to review what they heard during each session. Avoid filing away the notes until your exams. Get into the habit of reading through them regularly. This will certainly help you with revision before the end of term exams. We have a *closed* exam system at the college which means you are not allowed to refer to notes or books, so it's a good idea to review your lecture notes on a regular basis to prepare you for this method of assessment.

And one final point, a good number of our students record their lectures. This means that you can listen again later and a second listening can really clarify things. But mind your manners and be polite enough to ask the lecturer's permission before making your recording! Now, any questions before we move on to seminars?